Listening Lines

Staplehurst Stories

Volume Two

Compiled & Edited by Malcolm Buller

Layout & publishing by Andrew Buller - www.andrewbuller.co.uk

First published in Great Britain in 2024 - Text copyright © 2024 Malcolm Buller

Thank you to everyone who kindly provided images to accompany the stories featured in this volume.
Additional images on pages 8, 11, 100, 165, 166, 167, 169, 170, 172, 173 & 174 taken from Canva.com.

All rights reserved. No part of this publication may be reproduced, stored in a retrieval system, or transmitted, in any form or by any means, electronic, mechanical, photocopying, recording or otherwise, without the prior permission of the copyright owner.

Introductions

Malcolm Buller

Joan and I instigated Staplehurst Interest Group in March 2002 and the stories that we have heard over these years have fascinated us, but have reached a limited audience. The original idea for 'Listening Lines' then came from discussions with our son, Andrew. Telling stories of our childhoods are personal, but often they hold fascinating insights into life in different times and places. We realised that 'Listening Lines, Telling Tales' must surely apply to every community as it has since times before anything was written down. Every member of every village, town or city has a snippet at least that should be shared. Our twenty-first century generation are being reduced to text-limited bites of stories so this project can help redress the balance.

'Listening Lines – Staplehurst Stories' was the obvious place to start as our lines of communication were strongly established. The only stipulation was, and is, that the author lives, or has lived, in Staplehurst. Following its publication in November 2023, along with very positive reactions to the book, contributions started to arrive for a second volume and so 'Listening Lines – Staplehurst Stories – Volume 2' began in the Spring of 2024. Again, the lightest of editorial touches has been applied.

There are many links between the stories, their places and personnel, but there also contradictions. Even the most respected historians disagree, so it should be no surprise that we too have areas of doubt. We research where we can for factual accuracy, but I have never stipulated that any story must be true. Poetic licence can apply here.

October 2024

Joan Buller

When I had to take early retirement from my career as a primary school teacher due to serious mental health issues, I felt my life was over. I was desperate to replace this with something else meaningful. As my health slowly improved the Interest Group came into being. From a very shaky start I have grown in confidence again and I now have a lovely group of amazing friends. We laugh a great deal, which is the best medicine there is, and we all look out for and will help each other if needed. I am so grateful to all those who have attended over the years who have been my extended family and such a personal blessing to me.

October 2024

Please note that within this book you are directed to linked stories in the first volume by (LL-SS p***).

Author Notes

Joan and I arrived in Staplehurst, along with two toddlers, on David's first birthday, March 31st 1978. I was to teach at Headcorn Primary School and Joan began her involvement in the community by enrolling all the family in the library and attending toddler groups. She was soon on the Village Hall Playgroup Committee and attending every meeting of the Parish Council, before becoming a Councillor for forty years (LL-SS p235). I became involved with the Horticultural Society Committee, tennis coaching for children and joined badminton clubs, as well as judging flower shows around Kent. Joan returned to teaching in Staplehurst and my career took an even larger role when appointed a Head Teacher in Lamberhurst for eleven years.

Reassessing priorities when ill-health occurred meant early retirement from teaching for both of us and opportunities for new initiatives, especially as both sons left for university and independence. I attended art classes and Staplehurst Interest Group was born in the family home in 2002 in response to requests for daytime activities within the village. The weekly sessions followed whichever path the participants wanted and numbers attending grew until a hall space was needed rather than the lounge; for many years in the URC Schoolroom and then the Free Church. Visits, activities, discussions and speakers were all enjoyed. Such a wealth of talent does, and has, lived in our village and many unique tales have delighted us over these years.

With the 2020 pandemic lockdown, I found the urge to write. I had been helping our elder son by editing and advising on his children's book series, but as Andrew delved more into poetry, my latent interest was aroused. After publishing a poetic miscellany, a novel idea took over and self-editing skills were honed. Further poetry and a second novel have followed. In 2022 I formed the Staplehurst Library Poetry Group which meets monthly.

My other titles are all published by Andrew and available via Amazon UK. They are:-

- **What's in the Box?** – a poetical miscellany – poems written over time exploring many different styles
- **Parallel Lies** – a novel centred on three teenagers whose lives become inter-twinned in 1964 London – are untold truths really lies?
- **Leeds Castle – a poetic tour** – explores the 'loveliest castle in the world' and its grounds through many different poetic forms
- **Sitting in the Memory** – a novel exploring how simple events change the lives of family members
- **Listening Lines – Staplehurst Stories** – over fifty contributors and a hundred illustrations heralded this series of tales from distant memories to the present

"I received this as a Christmas gift. It's fabulous."
"What a present, what a revelation, what a book!"

Disclaimer

I must politely point out that readers should realise that I have no way of verifying the validity of the contributions by the past and present residents of Staplehurst. As someone, probably an editor, once said, "Don't let the facts get in the way of a good story!"

Contents

Route One	Malcolm Buller	1
Blaecca's Folk	Alan Baum	4
Crash Landing	Steve Heath	6
The Diary Of Freda Tomlin	Margaret Cramp	8
Bly Court Manor	Malcolm Buller	12
Light Relief	Steve Heath	15
The Local Government Act Of 1894	Malcolm Buller	17
Public Service	Eric Hotson	21
Conservation Area	Malcolm Buller	25
A Place To Remember	Tony Abrahams	29
From Pillar To Post	Bozena Sain	31
Where Are They?	Malcolm Buller	40
Practice Makes Perfect	Kate Minett	42
Bus Services In Staplehurst	Robin Oakley	48
A Vibrant Village	Grateful Resident	54
A Poetry Competition	Malcolm Buller	59
Poetry Group	Malcolm Buller	64
Woodcutter	Sue Terry	65
Is That Funny?	Anita Thompson	66
First Love	Moira Henderson	68
Out Of The Window	Anita Thompson	69
Why Staplehurst?	Interest Group Members	70
Shopping	Malcolm Buller	79
Guiding In Staplehurst	Annette Holmes	87
A Token Of Staplehurst	Malcolm Buller	91
Cricket In Staplehurst	A Cricketer	93

My Adventures	Chris Sharp	97
A Staplehurst Cricketer's Dream	Colin Breed	101
Staplehurst – A Dramatic Society	Dorothy Crooks & Lorna Manning	110
Retirement Home	Malcolm Buller	117
The Men's Shed	Richard James	120
Speed Watch	Malcolm Buller	126
A Yeoman's House	Anita Thompson	131
Living In History	Roy Laming	137
Play The Game	Malcolm Buller	145
If Only I Could	Laura Baker-Fawcus	148
Kick Off	Jess Burchell	151
A Train Crash	Malcolm Buller	154
Day To Day In Australia	Val Hoddinott	159
Journeys	Interest Group Members	164
Ron's Visit	Malcolm Buller	175
Joiners And Ceilers	Jean Smith	178
A Nature Reserve?	Chris Roome	186
Marden Road	Malcolm Buller	190
My Personal Journey	Silke Tetzlaff	195
Always Changing	Malcolm Buller	197
From The Garden	Malcolm Buller	202
Staplehurst School	Year 6 Pupils	204
Where Are They? – Answers	Malcolm Buller	210
Acknowledgements		214

Route One

Malcolm Buller

Julius Caesar came to Britain in 55BC, but left quite rapidly. He returned with a larger force of men to capture any settlement he came across. His messages back to Rome said that the residents were fierce, flesh-eating, skin-clothed savages. However, the evidence from that time shows that the people of Kent had artistic jewellery, gold, silver and tin coins as well as being expert potters, weavers and agriculturalists.

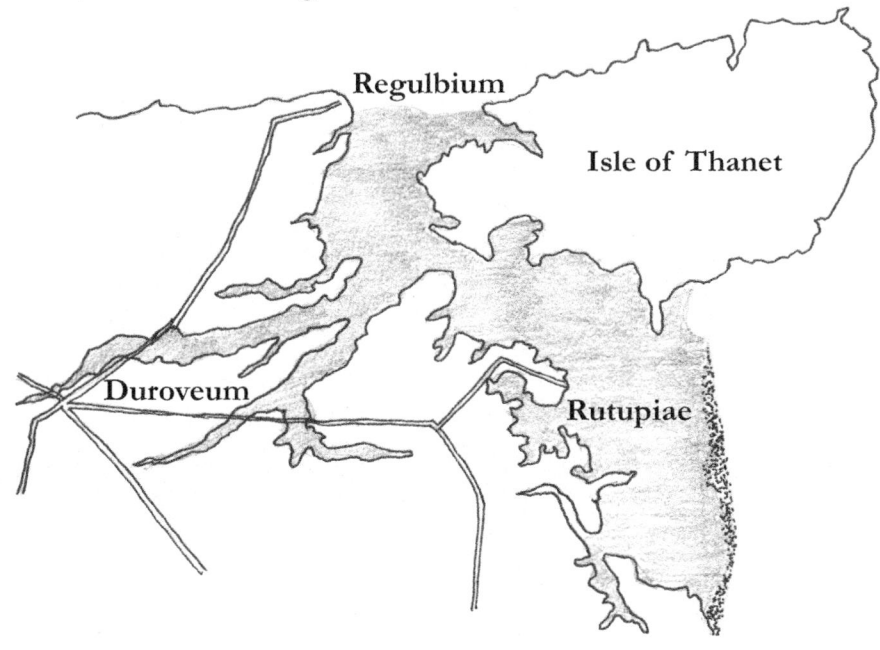

ROUTE ONE

The Roman conquest of Britain began in earnest in 43 AD after the short voyage across the narrow channel and landing in Rutupiae (Richborough) or at Regulbium (Reculver). Claudius's legions moved swiftly through the south east, establishing Watling Street, the major route to cross the rivers at Duroveum (Canterbury), Durobrivae (Rochester) and Londinium (London). Stone Street too linked strategic places. Moving troops and their support goods across differing terrains needed differing constructions of roads. Across boggy land a timber framework supported tree trunks, slabs of stone topped with gravel and pebbles. On drier land, drainage layers were topped with slabs and had kerbstones along the edges.

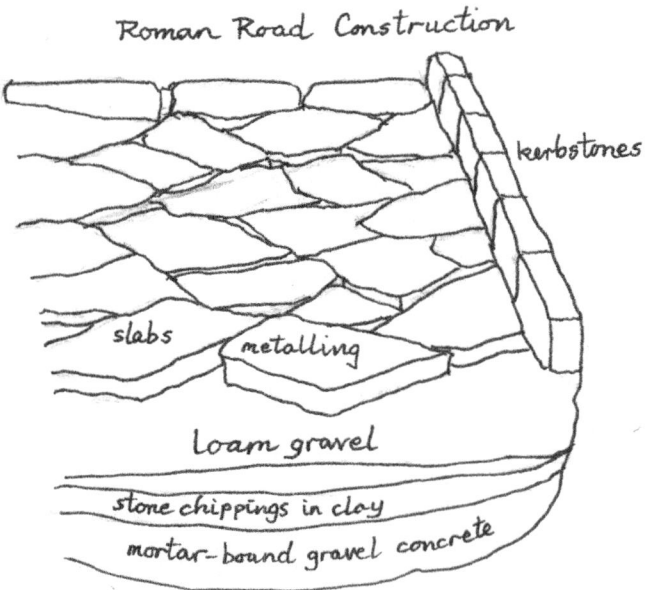

As the occupation objectives were achieved, further, more minor roads were constructed to widen the Roman web of control. From Durobrivae, Route I was built southwards towards Ore. It used natural channels through the chalk downs and skirted the River Medway before rising over the greensand ridges and through the densely forested lowlands of sticky clay. Minor rivers and streams could be bridged with the plentiful supplies of timber. After the Roman departure in 407 AD, a lack of maintenance under the rule of the Kings of Kent, saw the depreciation of this road network, especially under the Wealden mud. The hamlets and villages that had been served by this road still housed the Britons and their trading routes followed the established, often straight and shortest, tracks.

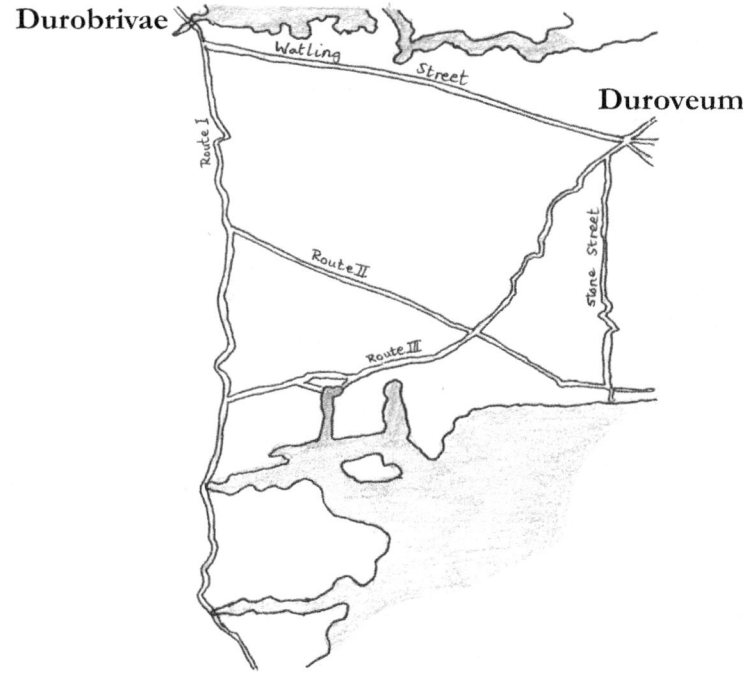

This north-south line is evident within and on both sides of our village. The A229, as we call Route 1, joins the line at the hamlet of Cross-at-Hand in the Maidstone Road, follows Station Road, the High Street and Cranbrook Road. However, taking the road north towards Chart Sutton, over the Grade II listed Hertfield Bridges, the Roman line is again clearly evident. To the south through Knoxbridge, the straight road encourages speeding modern motorists. Further stretches from Hawkhurst to Cripps Corner and Seddlescombe also show where Route I lies beneath. If only our modern road maintenance matched that of the Roman Empire!

Blaecca's Folk

Alan Baum

It seems that Chapel Lane was the centre of a very early community.

With all early histories, certainty is in short supply. Many accounts were written centuries later and archaeological evidence often contradicts previous 'knowledge'. The Jutes, like the Angles and Saxons, were Germanic who came across to Kent, the Isle of Wight and Hampshire, originally to help quell the Picts after the Romans left. The county was forested with plentiful water supplies and so clearings were made by over a hundred tribes to establish settlements. Early on, being close to an existing (minor) Roman road and a short distance from previously cleared land at Sutton Valence, made this a suitable place for the Blaecca tribe. By the ninth century there was a large area cleared for raising animals, especially pigs, which they drove to market along the ancient road.

As names are recorded over centuries, spellings alter. However, the addition of 'cot' to a family name, Blacecota, indicates that this was a manorial den. After the Norman Conquest, William put his half-brother, Odo, Bishop of Bayeux, in charge of Kent (to keep a close eye on him). Odo soon made-over to the archbishop from Leeds Manor the den of Blechecote, perhaps to unite them under the same lord as they shared the same drove. Bletchenden and Bletchingly add further evidence to show the spread of this kinship group.

The manor house which was built is now known as Bly Court Manor, but the plaque on the nearby cottages suggests yet another name for this historical centre of the village.

Crash Landing

Steve Heath

The Me 109 dived out of the sun on the evening of Saturday the 14th September 1940. Its target was the rear of a squadron formation of Spitfires. R6605 was hit and caught fire. Despite having been in plaster for nine months following a spinal fracture after crashing on take-off due to an engine failure in late 1939, and now having a wounded arm, Squadron Leader Robert Charles Franklin Lister bailed out successfully. His aircraft landed in Flat Field at the eastern end of Chapel Lane where it was later recovered by the 19 Maintenance Unit.

On the Sunday 22nd September Lister was attached to 92 Squadron at Biggin Hill where shortly afterwards he took command. On the 24th three squadrons were scrambled and met nine Ju88s, escorted by over a hundred Me109s. The squadrons broke formation and Lister was soon alone with nine 109s in pursuit. A canon shell penetrated the lower cockpit, badly injuring both of his legs and sending the aircraft into a spin. Managing to get back to Biggin Hill, he skidded into a diving turn which took the Spitfire into a valley below the airfield and stopped just a few yards from a wood.

Unable to fly again, Lister had many wartime roles in command at Biggin Hill, Alexandria, Haifa and Amman Jordan. He retired in 1954 and lived to reach the age of 84.

Flying Officer Robert Rutherford Smith came from London, Ontario, Canada to join the RAF in 1938. In 1940 he was involved in destroying enemy aircraft over Dunkirk to protect the escaping troops. On 15th September he was part of an attack on Do17s and Me110s over Sevenoaks when he was hit in his Hurricane V6616. He bailed out successfully, sending the aircraft to crash at Duckhurst Farm.

The site is given as Duckhurst Farm, Chapel Lane, Staplehurst. So it could be that Duckhouse Farm had some land at the end of Chapel Lane or was it a data error as Duckhouse Farm is in Clapper Lane?

The Diary Of Freda Tomlin

Margaret Cramp (nee Tomlin)

Freda was the eldest of four girls and one boy, living with their parents on a small farm called Lime Trees along the Marden Road (LL-SS p123). They all had chores to do, even Margaret as the youngest. During the Battle of Britain, Freda wrote her diary, recording first and second-hand experiences which, as father was also an ARP Warden, were quite reliable. The following are extracts of just a week of 'normal life in Staplehurst'.

THE DIARY OF FREDA TOMLIN

September 1940 – Amidst the Battle of Britain

Friday 13th

Air raid warnings had sounded nearly all day, but there were no sightings. Bombs were dropped on Biddenden Rd, Frittenden.

Saturday 14th

At 4.30pm we saw about 100 light bombers heading to London. George said as he put his hat on, "You never know what might come down." A few moments later we saw the smoke and flames from a Hurricane which had spun and crashed about half a mile north of Dunbury Farm, just over the Beult along the Chart Hill Road. A parachute from another was spotted as the pilot drifted to Hawkenbury where it was discovered he had been shot through the legs.

Sunday 15th

The siren sounded at about 11:30 and we heard terrific machine-gun fire, roarings and zoomings during the sermon. We exited church to see a lot of smoke from the station which was on fire. One of our planes had cut the tops off of pear trees growing opposite, gone right through the station and then the engine went on through Nolan's shed and finished up in Sorell's field. One wing landed on Station Cottages. The pilot, the booking-clerk and a plate-layer who was being served in the shop, were killed. The Station Master was injured, but not seriously.

A Spitfire came down just behind Duckhurst and burnt up, but the pilot bailed out. At 2pm the siren sounded again and I saw smoke rising from a plane which had crashed in the direction of Marden. We saw a parachute come down over the church and about four minutes later, three more towards Marden. Later we heard a roar and saw a bomber diving straight down over Pagehurst. We all ran indoors and there was a terrific bang. We saw a small cloud of black smoke about a hundred feet above our ploughed field. A bomber came down over Cranbrook and one parachute come down and another plane flying towards Maidstone, trailing smoke and with anti-aircraft guns firing at it. Smoke came from two others that had come down.

After the all-clear Betty and I went to view the station and heard another terrific bang and saw a cloud of smoke come from over Pagehurst way. We went round by the Plain Tavern and saw people picking up pieces of aeroplane for about a mile along that road. Another warning at about 7:15pm saw plenty of anti-aircraft fire, one large bomber with three Spitfires going round him. Mrs Moss said that 19 bombs had dropped on Mr. F. Tipples' Sweetlands Farm and they haven't exploded yet. Planes over and guns firing from 8:30pm until 6am.

Monday 16th

Sirens about 7:30am with 30 British fighters circling. We saw ten bombers at about 8:10 who, when they saw the fighters, turned and fled for the coast. Heard that a German airman had landed in Playfoot's field yesterday, but a second one's parachute didn't open. When Uncle Jack was playing golf at Bearsted yesterday another airman fell on the 13th fairway. He had a silver 'Iron Cross' and English money, but a non-opening parachute.

Tuesday 17th

During the afternoon raid a Spitfire came down on a barn at Folly Hill. Pilot Officer R.R. Smith, a Canadian with 229 Squadron, bailed out. Small enemy bombers were seen. Mr. Wendon told us that as he was feeding his chickens with Anthony Humphrey's help on Sunday, when a pilot of a Spitfire that went down at Pagehurst, landed on top of the hedge. He told them not to help him as he might be shot at up there. He was covered in oil and had a slight bullet wound in his leg. Also heard today that a time bomb had been dropped in the camp and another half a mile from the Lord Ragland and another in W. Tipples orchard at 2am.

Wednesday 18th

Had air-raids nearly all day. Saw a pilot bail out of a Spitfire this morning. He came down at Munn's Chickenden Farm and the plane at Bumpsteds, but didn't smash up as it was in a very slow spin. During the 1 o'clock raid we saw one man bail out, about twelve heavy bombers and fighters making skid-marks all over the sky. Heard terrific machine gunning from a cloud and a bomber came down with nine fighters around it. It came down at Colliers Street and wreckage strewn over two fields. Two more raids saw seventeen bombers and anti-aircraft fire.

Thursday 19th

Finished hop-picking at 1 o'clock having picked a total of 579 bushels. There was not much activity in the air until darkness fell, then 'Jerry' kept coming over just above the clouds and the anti-aircraft guns blazed away at him.

Bly Court Manor

Malcolm Buller

Delving into archives and reading accounts from many sources can lead to bewildering doubts or reveal fascinating stories. Bly Court Manor is one such tale where differences can add to speculation about the 'facts'. So many spellings of the same names add confusion.

Staplehurst marks the boundary between the Manor of Loddenden which was in the Hundred of Marden and the Den of Blecote which was in the Hundred of Cranbrook. Thus the church was in Cranbrook whilst the village was in the Marden Hundreds. This manor is mentioned in documents as Blechecot in 1180 and when the Bishop of London was patron as Lord of Staplehurst or Belcote. In the 13th and 14th centuries it is thought the De Sommery family lived here and may have been very influential in the founding of the church. Buildings were usually demolished when more modern ideas came along. The Manor of Staplehurst has been traced through the Cranbrook Hundred from the 15th century via the Fremingham, Pimpes, Isleys and Baker families. The present building dates from the 16th century and has been known as Blechecott, Blecourt, Blithecourt, Blay Court, Ble Court, Blecote, Blight Court, Blithe Court and Blececote, all of which probably derived from a Kentish folk name Bleccar.

BLY COURT MANOR

The Baker family had lived here since Henry VIII until the male line failed in 1661 when Sir John Baker, a member Privy Council, had four daughters who were his co-heiresses. In 1704, maps showed that the Blu Court estate was made up of 16 individual fields measuring 46 acres, all under the ownership of Robert Love. In the 18th century after sales and inheritances, Edmund Hungate Beagham possessed two thirds in trust of John Baker, Bridges Powell of one third in 1751. Then from 1754 John Austen owned the freehold until 1837. By 1842 Robert Shoobridge owned and lived in the Manor house with members of his family living in surrounding cottages under his name. Thomas Reeve purchased it in 1851 and lived there between 1852 and 1865.

The Poor Law Act came into effect in 1601, making it each parish's responsibility to find work for paupers. Furthermore, those within the parish who could afford to, should contribute to the upkeep of the poor. Butchers and greengrocers were to give cheaper food to the poor house whilst landowners should provide work for the unemployed poor. Parishes were to keep records and local landowners appointed overseers. In 1740 a Vestry meeting discussed the matter, but it wasn't until 1754 that Bly Court was obtained on a 21-year lease. The document shows the transfer from Mr Austen to James Suggle – butcher, John Bramley – yeoman, Edward Simmons – yeoman and Thomas Besley – churchwarden and overseer. The rent was £8 per year, paid half-yearly on feast days. Residents could give three months' notice to leave after 7, 11 or 14 years. It was proposed that it should be bought in 1838 for £250.

In 1809 the 44 Staplehurst 'Rules and Orders of the Poor House' were displayed and strictly enforced. The word of the Master and Dame was reported weekly on any misdemeanour by an inmate to the Churchwardens and Overseer who would take them before a magistrate to be punished for their 'crime'. No tea or liquor was to be taken into the house. All 'Poor Persons' must be daily employed in Work or Service. They must 'arise' by 5:30 in the winter and 5:00 in the summer half years. Those not attending Morning Service would lose their breakfast which would be broth, water-gruel, bread and cheese or any cold victuals not proper for dinner. Bad language by the Master or Dame would lose them 2/6d.

In 1829 the decline in the rural economy was exerting tremendous strain on the provision for the poor in mainly agricultural parishes. The Reverend T. W. Hornbuckle wrote to FitzHugh and Company in Liverpool seeking their help to convey a Staplehurst family to Quebec in Canada. The reply set out their fee of 5% and the cost for each adult and child for passage and provisions. It also mentioned that there was a "need for 10,000 labourers to build the Chesapeake and Ohio canal at wages between eight and twelve dollars for a month of 26 working days with food and good whiskey supplied". Edward Hickmott wrote to the Reverend from the ship 'City of Waterford' saying his family were waiting for a fair wind and that Mr Fitzhugh had paid the fees and there would be £9 for his family when they arrived in Quebec.

Light Relief

Steve Heath

Village life existed before electricity, but when it had arrived in the mid-1930s, it brought many expectations. Lighting main roads for the safety of residents came first, but the Parish Council was soon asked to provide lamps for minor roads too.

In March 1911 SPC had lobbied the Rural Sanitary Authority to 'make the road good' in Chapel Lane. Despite having no footpaths, eventually this cul-de-sac, which joins the High Street between the United Reformed Church (LL-SS p87) and the Royal Oak (a property that has changed name and usage over the years to be known as Bleu in 2024) was provided with two lights. These were placed at the junction outside the Chapel (LL-SS p90) and at the furthest visible point as a focus for the homeward travellers.

LIGHT RELIEF

A survey of parish assets brought the recommendation to the council that these two lights were beyond repair due to the condition of the pillars and the age of the wiring and connections and, as such, were dangerous. After much debate it was decided to have them dismantled, but not replaced. This horrified the residents and they attended meetings to alert the councillors to their fears for both security and the safety of residents and visitors. The quotes were re-examined, funding obtained and suitably-styled replacement columns and light fittings ordered. The Chapel Lane visitors and residents were pleased when modern LEDs lit up their way in 2021.

The Local Government Act Of 1894 – Is It Relevant Today?

Malcolm Buller

Royal Assent was given on March 5th to the 1894 Act of Parliament organising the country into Urban and Rural Districts. It also ensured that every rural parish with a population of over 300 would establish a Parish Council. The Act came into force on 3rd December and a special meeting was held in Staplehurst on Tuesday 4th December to receive nominations for Parish Councillors. Thirty-four candidates were nominated for the nine positions. Those elected were Reuben Baker, William Hoare, Henry Oyler, Robert Willsher Mannering, William Shoebridge, Jesse Norris, Charles Harris, John Jull and Frank Waters who all met for the first time on Monday 31st December 1894.

Parish Councils were entitled to hold their meetings within a room of Council-controlled Elementary Schools without charge. Amongst many proposals for the smooth running of the new Council, there was the decision to meet on the last Monday of each month, a request for improvements to the footpath in Bell Lane and another for residents to be encouraged to apply for allotments. At the following meeting there were many requests for several acres of land to be provided to hopeful individuals.

THE LOCAL GOVERNMENT ACT OF 1894

Tuesday 4 December 1894

At the first Parish Meeting for the parish of Staplehurst convened by the Overseers of the said parish to be held this day at half past six o'clock for the purpose of transacting the following business

(1) To elect a Chairman for the meeting
(2) To elect Parish Councillors

The notice convening the meeting having been read in which it was stated that the number of Parish Councillors to be elected was nine

It was proposed by the Rev. J. S. B. Chamberlain seconded by Mr Hoare

That Mr William Brooks be elected Chairman

It was proposed by Mr J. Norris seconded by Rev. J. Thatcher

That Mr Robert Barling be Chairman

The show of hands having been for Mr Barling 62 for Mr Brooks 31

Mr Barling then took the chair at a quarter to seven o'clock

The following nomination papers were then handed in to the Chairman and on being [opened?] the votes were as follows:—

Name of Candidate	No. of Votes
Baker Reuben	72
Beeching William	30
Burr William	
Forrister William	16
Grant Edwin Watson	14
Harris Charles	56
Hoare William	93
Jull John	48
Link George Thomas	9
Manwaring Robert Wiltshire	81

THE LOCAL GOVERNMENT ACT OF 1894

Very quickly the Parish was trying to obtain a public water supply and receiving comments about overgrown hedges and footpaths in need of surfacing (from ash to tar by the station). The provision of fire hydrants was raised, as was the failure of the Equitable Fire Office to pay the Fire Brigade for the use of their fire engine. The footpaths committee were empowered to repair the potholes in Bell Lane (and get a truck of ash if necessary). As the century changed it was noted that the Rural District Council had no reason to oppose the erection of the cheap dwelling houses that the Parish Council had referred to them.

In the Spring of 1949, Cranbrook Urban District Council gave a presentation to residents, suggesting that Staplehurst join them instead of being in the Maidstone Rural District Council. Was it a missed opportunity when the secret ballot revealed that Cranbrook got 25 whilst Maidstone received 39 votes?

The snippets above illustrate how very little has changed!

THE LOCAL GOVERNMENT ACT OF 1894

In 1994 and 2019, to celebrate the formation of our Parish Council, probably the first in Kent, anniversary celebrations were organised in the Old School halls where village organisations mounted displays of their activities. At the latter, all of the original leather-bound Minute Books, borrowed from the Kent Archives, were on display and all pages were photographed digitally so that the Council and Staplehurst Society Archives have these fascinating written records.

As the population has increased, so have the number of Councillors. Sadly, bureaucracy has shuffled down many responsibilities on to the shoulders of the parishes (LL-SS p28). As well as formal council meetings, there are many sub-groups formed and representatives found for other village organisations. Whilst at levels above, Councillors can earn by holding office and attending meetings, whilst being advised by many paid specialists, parishes are reliant on volunteers to undertake so many roles and employ their own staff to do everything else. In 2024, fifteen Staplehurst Parish Councillors were due to be elected. Only eleven candidates were nominated so these volunteers must share the extra burden.

Public Service

Eric Hotson

In 1946 I was born in Wisbech in Cambridgeshire, my father's home town, but soon afterwards the family moved to Brentford in Middlesex. After primary school I went to the local Secondary School where on the third day I met a girl called Janet. She was playing hockey and I was on the next field playing football. I wasn't brilliant at the academic side of school, but found success at all sports and I did end up as Head Boy.

My first job was as a clerk in the Land Charges Department of St Pancras Borough Council. I moved to the London County Council and having studied to do legal property work, I went into private practice in Twickenham before returning to local government at Southwark Council. Janet had been working at Mercedes Benz in Brentford before we married in March 1968. We bought a new semi-detached, three-bedroom house in Brooks Close, Staplehurst, for £4,250. Janet secured a post as secretary to a director at W R Balstons Paper Company in Maidstone and I continued to work in London paying £11.50 for my weekly season ticket. To avoid commuting I found a post in the legal department of Ashford Borough Council and either drove to work or caught the train. Janet was at home raising the family and after a couple

PUBLIC SERVICE

of years we moved to Westdene in Station Road. I was now working at Kingsford, Flower and Pain, Solicitors, who had pinched me from Ashford Borough Council.

My life outside work revolved around sport. Two days after arriving in Staplehurst I went to the cricket club and met Bill Tipples, the Chairman, who was mowing the ground. He signed me up and I went on to succeed him as Chairman. I then went to Maidstone Football Club and played for them for two years. I somehow found time to play squash at Hawkhurst. My last two football clubs were the village team and, on Sundays, Diagrit here in the village.

One evening there was a knock at the door and a stranger asked if I would be a candidate to be a Borough Councillor for the village as I was well-known for cricket and football and for frequenting the Railway Tavern. I had never been a member of any political party, but I agreed to give it a go. I had been given leaflets to distribute and on election night I lost by 4 votes. Ann Widdecombe, our Member of Parliament, (LL-SS p224) demanded a recount. After the recount, I lost by 2 votes. I stood a year later and wrote my own leaflets which brought success. During the next 20 years, through seniority, I became Leader of the Conservative Group on Maidstone Borough Council, Leader of the Council and Mayor. Being Mayor was a wonderful experience. Janet and I visited so many worthwhile people doing marvellous things for their groups and communities. I raised a record sum of money for my chosen charities, Maidstone Young Carers and the Kent Air Ambulance.

I became a County Councillor, again through a knock on the door. I enjoyed representing 7 adjoining Parish Councils for 16 years and becoming Chairman of Kent County Council which was a great honour. During my above roles I met many members of the Royal family, including Queen Elizabeth and the Duke of

PUBLIC SERVICE

Edinburgh, Prince Charles and Princess Anne. Highlights were attending Garden Parties at Buckingham Palace.

Trying to work full time alongside Borough and County commitments was becoming difficult so I stepped down as Borough Councillor as my firm wanted me to open an office in Bank House, Staplehurst as I had many local clients. I was with Kingsford, Flower and Pain for 33 years and Janet was School Secretary for 33 years at New Line Learning, the school where many Staplehurst children attended.

PUBLIC SERVICE

Our parents have lived with us at Westdene, Highbury and finally at White Willows and our three girls lived in the village for all their teenage years. Reflecting now on fifty-six years of life in Staplehurst shows me how welcoming the Jack Blunts, Bill Tipples and Herbert Thirkells (LL-SS p13) of the village were to newcomers. Getting involved from the very earliest days has meant that Janet and I have made so many friends.

Modern life suggests that so many are too busy, but quality of life comes from involvement.

Conservation Area

Malcolm Buller

The notion that areas of cities, towns and villages being in need of conservation had no legitimacy in law until the Civil Amenities Act of 1967. The need to rebuild after the Second World War was clear, but some of the results are somewhat obvious to us now. Since 1990, the Planning (Listed Buildings and Conservation Areas) Act places the duty on local authorities to designate these areas where they are appropriate.

CONSERVATION AREA

A Conservation Area is "an area of architectural or historic interest, the character and appearance of which it is desirable to preserve or enhance". Such designation gives extra authority to control any demolition of unlisted buildings, more restricted permitted development rights for single dwellings and the protection of trees. Without preservation or enhancement of the special character, developments should be refused planning permission.

The Staplehurst Conservation Area was designated on November 26th 1987 by Maidstone Borough Council. It largely encompasses the original heart of the village surrounding the High Street. It stretches from the north at the old school site and Surrenden to South View on Church Hill and stops at the edge of the Frittenden Rd. The Chapel Lane area is also included, but the School, Library and Parade are not. Contained within it are many Listed Buildings, including the Grade 1 church, Grade 2* Loddenden Manor and many Grade 2s. In addition, other places can be identified as a Non – Designated Heritage Asset (NDHA) and there are many of these in our village. MBC have a duty to regularly review such areas through consultation, the last of which took place in early 2024.

CONSERVATION AREA

Many residents may be unaware of many of these gems as they walk along the High Street from the Old School – NDHA, and pass Oaks Farmhouse – G2, Oaks Farm Barn – NDHA, Loddenden Manor Railings and Gates – G2, Loddenden Manor – G2*, North and South Cottages – G2, Little Loddenden – G2, Sycamore Cottage – NDHA, Little Loddington House (parade of shops) – NDHA, United Reformed Church – NDHA, Minton House – G2, Crampton – G2, 1,2,3 Crown Cottages – G2, Butchers – G2, Wimborne House – G2, Hill House, steps and railings – G2, Aysgarth – G2, Opticians – G2, 1,2,3 Church Cottages – G2, All Saints' Church G1, many G2 tombs, Staplehurst House and Old Rectory – NDHA and the Parish Rooms – NDHA, every one of which has a fascinating history.

Returning you also find many of the terraced dwellings are grouped, as in centuries gone by they were probably single buildings. Look out for the old Firemark under the overhang on the South View trio – G2, Rosemary to Kent Cottage – G2, Bell Cottage, steps and handrail – G2, King's Head – G2, shop and house adjoining – G2, house and shop – G2, Vine House – G2, Railings – G2, Lime Terrace – G2, Green Court and Green Court Cottage – G2, Drey Cottages – G2, Saddlery and Little London Cottage – G2, Chestnut Cottage and Chemist – G2, The

CONSERVATION AREA

Bower – NDHA and Surrenden – G2. Along Chapel Lane, the Chapel House and Providence Baptist Chapel are G2, followed by Bly Court Manor – G2.

The conservation area has essential edges of trees and hedges which soften the street scene. Furthermore, all vegetation adds to the quality of the air and reduces pollution from passing traffic. Pedestrians too are separated from traffic and enjoy the beauty of growing plants. The surrounding environment enhances the setting of the listed buildings and NDHAs.

As the years pass, names may change, but alterations to the buildings are under scrutiny. The saddlery existed for many decades until it changed to a nursery school, but how many busy people have seen the holes above its door for ventilation? Children in Year 3 used to be taken on 'Spotting Trails' when Joan was their teacher.

A Place To Remember

Tony Abrahams

It was 1972 when I was looking for somewhere to live near Staplehurst Railway Station to enable me to commute to London for an eighteen-month stint. I wanted an older property that needed work doing to it, but goodness knows why. Low and behold, one came up in Station Road, next-door-but-one to the sub post office. Built in 1892, it had gas lighting, just one fractured cold-water tap, no bathroom, an outside loo and a brass name on the front gate. It had been owned by a partially blind lady and the garden was completely overgrown. Does anyone remember it from those days? My employers surprisingly gave me a mortgage and the council a very generous improvement grant. Six months later it was habitable.

Our two boys were having the time of their lives and with Simon's birthday coming up, we sent a lovely card of Kent Oast Houses to Ed Stewpot's Junior Choice on Saturday morning radio. Ed would give out birthday greetings to the listeners, but he kept on talking about our address throughout the programme; so our friends told us! Yes, you guessed it, we missed the broadcast. However, the Kent Messenger (or Kentish Express) came, took a photo of the kids and wrote an article about this strange name.

A PLACE TO REMEMBER

Within a few days, letters, phone calls and visits were numerous. The suggestions for its origins were largely either, a man had the house built and on moving in he said to his wife, "Here-U-R-Then" or the paper boy used to chuck the paper over the hedge and call out, "Here-U-R-Then!". If you believe either of these then great, but if you think you know better, please feel free to get in touch with the editor!

Another house name in Staplehurst caught the Editor's eye.

From Pillar To Post

Bozena Sain

Stanislav (Stan) Dzieglewski was a Polish soldier in the 1920 war against Bolshevik Russia. He was rewarded with a plot of land in the village of Sztun in the east of Poland near Wolyn. In 1937 he married Antonia (Tosia) Chocianowski from Odessa who was a talented teacher. On the 3rd June 1939, their only daughter, Bozena Maria, was born in a tiny room in Warsaw. Grannie, Mother, Aunt Nacia and the baby hired a holiday chalet near Klembow. With many doubts, towards the end of August, mother and baby returned to Sztun and parted with Nacia in Warsaw.

Tosia in her One Teacher School

FROM PILLAR TO POST

On the 1st September 1939, Nazi Germany invaded Poland. Thousands fled towards the east, many to Wolyn. The farm was filled with tired travellers, hungrily fed from Tosia's camp kitchen.

On the 17th September, Stalin's Soviet Red Army invaded Poland from the east. Local Ukrainians in Wolyn were incited to kill any Poles. The family were well-loved in Sztun and left unharmed, though thefts of food and belongings by the Red Army's undisciplined soldiers were tolerated as being shot was the alternative.

At 2am on 10th February 1940, Communists gave the family 25 minutes to gather belongings before being taken away. Stan loaded hidden food into a chest and on to a cart. The chickens were killed and flung on too. Tosia was urged by the Communist Officer to take everything so gathered warm clothing, crockery, utensils and bedding which left with them on the cart. Their expectation was to be shot. They were loaded with hundreds of others into waiting cattle trucks.

Tosia and Bozena were put on a high seat above Stan and his young brother Adas, sitting on the chest. Seven more families were squeezed in. There was a single stove for heat and cooking in the sub-zero temperatures. Tosia rationed the food and shared it. The train stopped at tiny stations or in the countryside when those alive could stretch their limbs whilst the dead were removed from the trucks. After this short interval, a whistle blow signalled the train to start, resulting in a scramble to regain their sanctuary from the bitter weather. The journey took two months to reach Archangel inside the Arctic circle and onwards to Jozma near to Pinega. Thirty kilometres in trucks brought the survivors to the labour camp, deep in the forest, whilst the elderly and sick were put on sleds to be exposed to the elements on which many died.

One elderly survivor found her sister had perished and Tosia persuaded Stan to dig a shallow grave in the frozen earth, for which Tosia was given the warm, snow-proof boots which prevented frostbite. These later arrivals were told that the earliest had been forced to live in the forest whilst they cleared the land for the camp and built all of the huts for the soldiers before starting those for the prisoners. Immediate disorientation showed that escape was futile. Adas was sent to log trees, but Stan's beard made him appear much older so he was allowed to remain.

Tosia became the spokesperson for the Poles in the camp as she could speak Russian to the Commandant. He blustered as he listened to ensure he was towing the expected line of harshness, but quietly softened a few things that wouldn't be noticed. Having a small child stopped Tosia from forest work so was told to clean the latrines to 're-educate' her. Occasional visits from local Russians showed how poor they were so Tosia's store of crockery and clothes could be exchanged for some meagre food items. Bozena was sent to the local creche where they served a warm soup each day which supplemented the meagre helping of black bread. However, she also received doses of every childhood illness. The prayer, 'Give us this day our daily bread' meant everything to the men rationed to 400 grams and women 300 grams of bread a day. Occasional parcels would arrive from her sister which gave bartering power. A thin spread from a small bottle of melted butter helped Bozena digest her ration. Even so, Bozena's cries kept everyone awake until they were sent to sleep in the camp kitchen.

Three months of bitter darkness in the middle of a long winter took its toll. The other seasons were short, but the forests sprouted many welcome berries to be devoured and saved, being such a boost of vitamins. Wolves and bears roamed here too, not willing to share their crops. Autumn brought protein from mushrooms which were pickled, dried, salted, smoked and stored for the harshness to follow.

Bozena caught every illness, yet survived. It seemed that the small, skinny ones faired far better than those who arrived chubby. After the second bout of diphtheria, Tosia lay awake on the straw mattress on the floor that they all shared. She heard the howling wind, saw the snow falling and heard the heavy footsteps on the wooden floor, stop by the kitchen door. She screwed her eyes tight as a figure bent over her and a Russian voice told her, "All that has happened to you, had to happen, but nevertheless you will survive and live." He added, "Budit zyt! – You'll live!" The howling wind echoed the words as it blew out of a crack in the pane and she opened her eyes to see only the blizzard. She was convinced that it was the ghost of Stalin, even though he was still alive.

And so it came to pass that in late June 1941, Hitler's troops attacked Russia. Stalin asked for help from Britain and General Sikorski, leader of the Polish Government-in-exile. On 16th August a general amnesty for the Poles was declared, with the men immediately released and sent to join the Polish Army under General Anders. Adas came to tell his family the news. When Stan asked the Commandant for permission to leave the camp, he denied knowing about the amnesty. Tosia went every day, read the Russian notices and asked for permits to leave, spreading the word throughout their compatriots. Many thought it was a trap. Eventually summoned by the Commandant, the family were given their papers to sign. A few days later they, and just five others from the 250 families, were taken to Pinega and on to Archangel. At last they were free!

The destination was Buzuluk, but the train was crammed with people except for one carriage which the family eagerly entered, not knowing it was reserved for Russian Officers. Stan was to be thrown from the speeding train by one, but fellow officers saved him by kicking him and ejected them all into the corridor to join the masses elsewhere. Each journey was short and waiting for space on the next train, finding food and shelter constant problems. When they got to Gorki, Tosia remembered Mucha, her schoolfriend and sought her out. Luckily she couldn't as Poles were regarded as spies and contact would have brought disaster for Mucha's family. When she returned, Stan had got tickets on a steamer travelling south along the Volga River to Kuybyshev. They marvelled at the beauty and sights from the crowded top deck.

After many weeks of travel, a train of sardined refugees arrived in Buzuluk. Adas left them to join the army whilst the Polish Consulate was the destination families went to, as well as to the International Red Cross. Stan was put in charge for the next journey, but Bozena caught measles so Tosia and Bozena had to get off at Tashkent and find the children's hospital. No visiting meant a daily list of children's temperatures was posted. Tosia dreaded Bozena's name not being on it. She demanded to see the Head Nurse and Doctor. She refused to leave without giving a blood transfusion to the daughter she could barely recognise. Her determination saved Bozena who was able to leave ten days later. Tosia rented a corner of a Russian family's veranda for Stan's bread ration. He got a job for the Polish Delegation so obtained some coupons for a soup kitchen.

Every little while they moved in search of work and therefore food. Tosia had to carry Bozena who was too weak to walk. They got lost and Tosia rested on the long veranda of an old wooden building whilst Stan searched on. When the proprietor arrived, he courteously told her it was an Uzbek inn and he was preparing for a function for men only so they had to leave. As she rose, it began to rain and the old man said she could stay until before the guests arrived. She watched him sweep the large room, arrange cushions around a square sunken centre and light a stove in the middle.

Tosia tried to stay out of sight as the guests were greeted by their host. He asked where Stan was, but she knew not. Looking at the heavier rainfall, the guests agreed that she could stay until he came. Her smile conveyed her heartfelt thanks as she cuddled Bozena to her for warmth. But then she was jolted into remembering that they had eaten nothing all day by the smell of roasted meat, tantalizingly wafting over her. She focussed on the path through the rain, searching for Stan's approach. She had to glance in and saw two boys carrying a huge tray with white rice and meat to the seated men with their legs warming in front of the fire. Her hunger clawed at her spirit as she stared through the rain. The old Uzbek host placed a large bowl of hot food beside her and the smiling guests motioned to her to eat. Tears of joy thanked them as Bozena and she enjoyed the best meal ever. When Stan finally returned, he too was similarly supplied.

As the host was locking up Stan asked if he knew of anywhere where they could spend the night. After a moment, he said they could use the shed where his brother usually kept his two donkeys. They could use the straw in the corner. He also found a coverlet as the night would be chilly. As Tosia lay awake, she could see twinkling stars through small holes in the roof and thought through the events of that day; through despair and hunger to kindness and nourishment. She wanted to treasure this day so worked out the date it must be. As she cradled her baby, lying in a stable beside an inn, she realised that it was December 24th, Christmas Eve!

Stan finally got the job of Information Officer for the Polish Delegation in Tashkent. With his white and red armband, he met every train of Polish refugees, telling them where to register and how to get their food ration. One day he returned home early with incredible news. Tons of food, medical supplies and clothes had arrived from India and the Polish Government and Red Cross Expedition would take back 150 young Polish orphans. They needed qualified nurses and teachers to accompany them. Tosia's documents had been stolen, but Stan had safely kept her teacher's membership card. When she was interviewed, the professor was sceptical. The elegant young woman in the photograph did not resemble the gaunt figure in rags before him. His questions were designed to trick her, but her in-depth knowledge convinced him she was the teacher and hadn't stolen the card.

Dr Konarski examined every child to be taken to India. Tosia listed all of Bozena's illnesses and the measles in particular worried the doctor. When she asked him for the truth, he said Bozena had only six months to live and that if she did, she would get tuberculosis. Tosia begged for medicines, but there were none. He prescribed double rations of milk and fruit. So, at two and a half, with no hair or teeth, unable to stand, let alone walk, Bozena was carried to the train to leave Russia and her father behind. Along with the orphans, they travelled in a convoy of army trucks through Persia and onwards to India. Stan didn't know, but he had already contracted typhoid. In hospital he was brought hot broth every day by a Jewish lady whose life had been saved by the bread tokens Stan had helped her obtain. So many more did not survive these outbreaks.

Bozena did survive and later met Dr Konarski in India. She lived in Staplehurst from 1987 until 2021, when she left to live in Italy near to her son and his family. As well as many friends, she has left behind her wonderful book in Staplehurst Library (LL-SS p158). The above is a snapshot of chapter four in Russia.

FROM PILLAR TO POST

Life in India, Lebanon and Australia are yet to come in this tale of courage and survival. Despite everything, Tosia survived to be 95 years old.

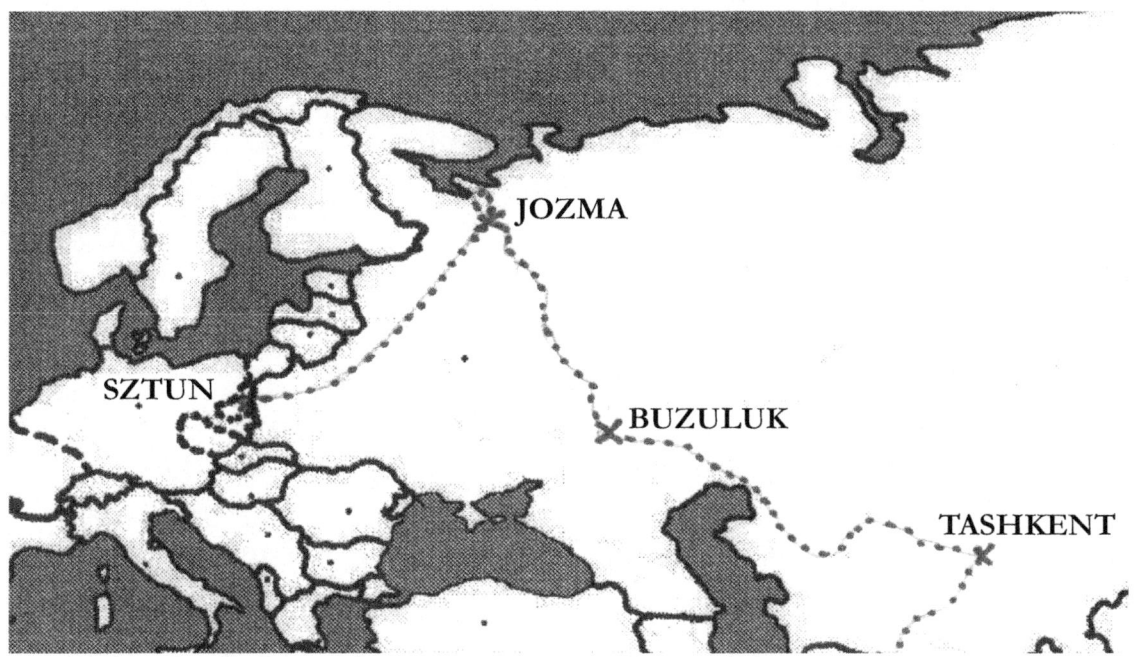

Where Are They?

Malcolm Buller

These could all be found in Staplehurst in 2024. Some have been here for centuries and some for decades, but will they survive the march of time? Many have stories and some mysteries. Do you know where they are and what they signify? Answers are near the end of this book.

1
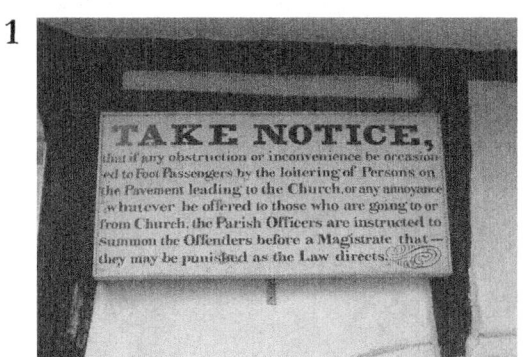

2

3

4

WHERE ARE THEY?

5

6

7

8

9

10

Practice Makes Perfect – GP Memories

Kate Minett

I have lived in Staplehurst for 35 years. My late husband was a GP for 25 years. For most of that time he was based at Marden Medical Centre, a practice that covered Staplehurst.

PRACTICE MAKES PERFECT

Nigel started in General Practice in 1986. His predecessor introduced him to the routine, surgeries morning and evening with home visits during the afternoons. There was no appointment system, it was first come first served, so a queue would form long before the surgery opened. Nigel was amused to hear that the outgoing doctor had several elderly ladies he would visit monthly for a sherry! Post surgery was time used to update records, complete hospital referrals and wash returned pill bottles to be reused filling new prescriptions. A computer system was being introduced and every 'Lloyd George' patient record had to be read and the past medical history entered onto it. This threw up some amusing old letters – I still have one from a dermatologist at Maidstone Hospital from the 1960's. A patient had been referred to him with a large wart and the consultant suggested his treatment should be 'to apply copious amounts of morning spital' to resolve the issue.

There were no mobile phones, just a bleep system, so the patients would ring our home when Nigel was on call. I would bleep him if he was out visiting and he would take his collection of 10p coins and try and find a phone box or ask permission of a homeowner to use their phone to pick up the message. I can't remember exactly when the first 'mobile' phone arrived in the practice, but I do remember it was the size of a large briefcase. From its introduction I was free to concentrate on our growing family. However, if Nigel was called out to an emergency at night, I would have to answer any calls that came through. I have mild dyscalculia and so had a habit of transposing the digits of telephone numbers or, as on one memorable occasion, sent Nigel to bang on the door of number 23 instead of 32 at 3am. An angry head popped out of the bedroom window, but once they realised it was Nigel, cheerfully pointed him to the correct address.

The Senior Partner at that time was experienced in home births and had his own pair of obstetric forceps. He flourished these at me when I was 9 months pregnant with our first child and volunteered to 'help out' if needed. Thankfully our first child arrived without the aid of such intervention. One of Nigel's patients was unhappy that he had cancelled his surgery and chosen to be with me during the delivery. He was quoted asking, 'Where's Minett?' When the situation was explained he complained loudly that Nigel should 'be here to see me' and not at the hospital!

The life of a GP used to be far more integrated with the local community, sharing in both joys and sorrows. We attended many weddings and christenings. Nigel was invited to judge bonny baby competitions, dog shows, open fetes and the like, was asked to speak at events and even led two funeral services.

When I was still involved in taking calls, I could be aware of an individual's circumstances, but patient confidentiality meant Nigel would never discuss what was revealed in consultations. It was interesting that many people assumed he did, which could be tricky. I was often in trouble with friends who felt I was not showing sympathy for issues I knew nothing about.

PRACTICE MAKES PERFECT

Nigel regularly got stopped in the street to discuss medical issues when he was off duty. He struggled to cope with this until the Senior Partner suggested he just ask the enquirer to drop their trousers in the middle of the pavement to indicate how inappropriate these approaches were, though Nigel was never able to bring himself to follow this advice! Patients would knock on our door when we lived in Marden and would regularly comment on his purchases in the local stores, criticising his choice of take away as unhealthy or tutting if he was buying a bottle of wine. This prompted our move to Staplehurst which led to far fewer disturbances.

It was a frequent occurrence to get a telephone call in the middle of the night to inform him that the burglar alarm was going off at the surgery. Once we had been there earlier in the evening for a leaving party and two hours after we had gone to bed a call came through. When he went to check, a helium balloon left bobbing around the waiting room was found to be the culprit. Another time we had been at a party, so I had to drive him over to check the premises. He made me promise to stay in the car for my own safety and then moments after he entered the building, he let out a blood curdling yell! I was at first terrified – and then very angry – when after a few minutes he came back out to say he had decided to shout as loudly as he could to make sure the culprit was no longer in the building!

Over the years there were many memorable moments. Nigel went out to visit a patient with abdominal pain and fearing appendicitis, knelt on the bed to better examine her tummy. Before he knew it, he was sprawled across her. The patient had omitted to tell him she had a waterbed! Fortunately, despite her pain, she found the episode funny. Once one mother told him quite proudly, that she was taking the contraceptive pill in the belief it would stop her daughter getting pregnant. He was called out to a lady who had been hit by lightning. She survived, apparently saved by her underwired bra which disseminated the shock away from her heart. On smashing up his new car when called out urgently in the snow in 1987, he was not amused to find the 'urgent' call was a patient suffering from a mild rash. After putting my car in a ditch on a flooded road a few weeks later when the snow melted and having to be pulled out by a local farmer, I had to live with the smell for months!

When we found out to our surprise I was expecting a fourth child, one of his favourite farmers called him into her kitchen after he had visited her husband. She produced a large carving knife from a drawer and suggested quite strongly to Nigel that he needed to take measures to ensure that our family was complete, otherwise she would offer to do the job herself. Nigel found this very funny, but perhaps there was a little concern as he did have a vasectomy shortly after!

Nigel loved people and he loved his job. Always keen to give his best, his surgeries regularly overran with the reception staff having to bear the brunt of the complaints. Somehow, by the time patients actually made it in to see him, no one complained as they realised that they had his full attention. Patients were incredibly appreciative; I still have boxes of thank you letters and cards that people wrote to him and he was showered with gifts at Christmas.

When invited to share a story for this second edition of 'Listening Lines' it was suggested that I write about the fundraising I have been involved in for Pancreatic Cancer UK since my husband's brief illness and death in 2012 at the age of 54. I do not feel I have done anything remarkable and would rather honour Nigel's memory with this little piece. I am proud to mention that as a family we have now raised in the region of £50,000 for research and support of those affected by this disease and take comfort from the hope that a breakthrough in early detection will come.

Bus Services In Staplehurst In The 1960's

Robin Oakley

I have been a bus and railway enthusiast since around the age of 12. Then, my idea of fun would be to spend the day trainspotting on Clapham Junction Station or bus spotting at Victoria Coach Station.

DH159 HKE867 - Bristol K6A new in 1945 with wartime utility bodywork, rebodied in 1953 with Weymann H30/26R bodywork.

BUS SERVICES IN STAPLEHURST

I was one of the earliest members of the Maidstone and District & East Kent Bus Club with an interest in buses throughout Kent, so when I married Beryl and we moved to a new house in Staplehurst (3-bedroom costing £3,045) in 1963, I soon purchased a Maidstone and District bus timetable for 1/- (5p) which ran to 340 pages. I recently discovered it in a box of bus ephemera and thought it would be interesting to compare the bus services through Staplehurst in 1963 with what we have today (when the service is not the Covid-19 version).

The bus services were the number 5 from Maidstone to Hastings which interworked with the 57 Gravesend to Hastings and the 44 Maidstone to Frittenden, operated by M & D buses from garages at Gravesend, Knightrider Street Maidstone, Hawkhurst and Hastings. The journey time from Staplehurst to Mill Street Bus Station in Maidstone was 27 minutes compared with the now, Station Road to King Street which is 28 minutes, on a good day. The first bus to Maidstone was at 06:46 compared currently with 07:24 on a non-school day. There were 20 buses a day between Maidstone and Staplehurst on weekdays and 14 on Sundays in 1963 compared with 16 on school-days, 11 on Saturdays and none on Sundays or Bank Holidays in 2024.

SO43 LKT991 - Bristol L6A new in 1950 with Eastern Coachworks B35R bodywork

During the morning peak, three buses from Maidstone terminated at Staplehurst Quarter, turning by reversing into Pinnock Lane, a somewhat hazardous manoeuvre as Hanmer Way did not exist then. Buses terminated at Mill Street Bus Station which faced on to Palace Avenue where the small car park is now. They reversed into the stands to load their passengers, but this congestion caused in Palace Avenue had resulted in a second bus station being opened at the opposite end on the corner of Lower Stone Street. There was an access to and from this into the rear of the Maidstone garage which was part of the Knightrider House Head Office complex. The last bus out from Maidstone each evening was at 22:20, but in 2024 these are at 18:17, or 18:27 on a Saturday.

DH478 VKR470 - AEC Regent V new in 1956 with Park Royal H33/26RD bodywork, one of M&D's first batch of double-deckers with doors on the rear platform.

BUS SERVICES IN STAPLEHURST

For anyone wishing to travel on the 57 to Gravesend the journey took 98 minutes and to Hastings 106 minutes including 7 minutes waiting time for connections at Hawkhurst Bus Station. The buses operated on the route were double-deckers, mostly half-cab with a rear entrance, although rear-engined Leyland Atlanteans and Daimler Fleetlines with front entrances were becoming the company's bus-of-choice as they could be one-man-operated. The M & D bus livery was green and cream and for coaches it was cream with green decoration. Bus overhauls and major repairs were carried out at the company's works which were situated in Postley Road, Maidstone, the site of which is now occupied by houses.

Tuesdays must have been exciting if you lived in Frittenden as the Tuesdays Only single-deck, one-man operated service 44 ran to Maidstone for market-goers via Staplehurst, Marden Thorn, Marden and Stile Bridge.

90 390 DKK - AEC Reliance new in 1958 with Harrington Wayfarer C41F bodywork, subsequently modified to become dual purpose coach/bus in 1963.

BUS SERVICES IN STAPLEHURST

M & D express coach services called at Staplehurst for pre-booked passengers on their route E2 between Tenterden, Cranbrook and Victoria Coach Station in London. The journey took 140 minutes so it was not surprising that when the railway was electrified and trains ran to a regular interval timetable, express coach services became less popular and finally ceased. In 1996 the day return railway fare between Staplehurst and London Charing Cross was around 19/- (95p). M & D coastal express services E8 and E21 called at Staplehurst once a day on their routes between Gillingham and St. Leonards and Eastbourne during the summer months. Bus services carried unaccompanied parcels between agents in most villages and small towns. Staplehurst had three parcel agents. C.E. Goodsell was opposite the butchers, J. Forster at The Quarter Stores (now demolished) and V. Gibson at the Stores on the corner of Market Street (now the Kebab Shop).

The increase in rail travel and car ownership have resulted in changes in bus services and their infrastructure. Both of the Maidstone bus stations have gone although it is still possible to see the Mill Street bus office and waiting room as part of the coffee bar at Tenterden Station on the Kent and East Sussex Railway. The Knightrider Street bus garage has been replaced by one in Armstrong Road, and that at Hawkhurst has been replaced by a supermarket.

M & D became part of the National Bus Company on January 1st 1969, but was privatised on 7th November 1986 to a management-led team through a holding company called Einkorn Limited. During the period 1995-1998 various changes of management and ownership took place until M & D became part of the Arriva Group of transport companies. This in turn was bought out by the German railway company Deutsche Bahn (DB) and traded as Arriva Kent and Surrey. DB owned over 4,700 buses across the country, but in 2023 it sold Arriva to a US private equity infrastructure firm called I Squared for £1.4 billion. In

February 2024, Arriva in Kent had a fleet of 256 buses shared between Maidstone, Gillingham, Tunbridge Wells and Northfleet depots.

Some Reflections Of Staplehurst – A Vibrant Village

A Grateful Resident

Where do you begin to describe a village like Staplehurst? The variety and number of organisations and establishments offering all sorts of ways to engage in village life and the sheer number of people who give freely of their time to run them. Well, I don't know and so I am simply, without mentioning any names, going to list some of the memories I have from those from which I have benefitted or in which I have participated in some small way and those which I have watched in awe as they are provided week after week.

I suppose my first involvement was with the PTA and their various entertainments. Two in the early years I remember which were new innovations at the time were firstly, a Frustration Forum. This was a stall we had at the Annual Carnival and Fete where you threw balls at people's old and broken crockery rather than coconuts; and very popular it turned out to be. The second were Monte Carlo evenings, especially the first one which took place in the South Eastern Pub which really gave the right ambience for the evening. You gambled the night away with monopoly type money which you bought with real money; the exchange rate for which was very generous!

A VIBRANT VILLAGE

Mentioning the Carnival and Fete brings to mind the time when, for many years there was a procession of floats around the village and many of the organisations participated, generally on vehicles kindly supplied by local businesses (LL-SS p63). One year in particular I recall Eagle Cub Pack portraying Jungle Book. This huge lorry turned up (they look so vast when empty) and we wondered how we were going to fill it. But plenty of greenery was found, the kids suitably dressed and painted; and it looked great. We were fortunate that the procession for a number of years passed our front door and so we could sit on the lawn and cheer them on, with a glass of something!

Very recently there were those wonderful Fireworks evenings with the impressive bonfires, not to forget the French Markets and Christmas Carols on the Parade. Of course, you can't mention Christmas without Santa touring our village every year and the magnificent Christmas Star which shines out over the Weald from the tower of All Saints Church over the Advent and Christmas season. I was privileged to assist in putting it up for several years and what an exciting time that was, especially hauling the star up the side of the tower, with the customary cake and coffee afterwards in one of the Church Cottages.

All the Churches between them, as well as their regular services and related groups, offer a wide variety of other events for the village throughout the year, often for charitable purposes including coffee mornings, musical evenings, talks, quizzes and a variety of special services around the celebration of Christmas and Easter; something for everyone (LL-SS p83). They have also worked together for decades now, sharing services, delivering Christmas and Easter cards to every house in the parish as well as carrying out the annual Christian Aid collection. Also, on Good Friday, they give Witness on the Parade offering hot cross buns with serviettes giving an Easter message to those who pass by. They have a cake and coffee stall at the village carnival each year and have helped at some recent Parish Picnic events on the Surrenden Field. They have also organised a number of public events, the most ambitious one being the Village Celebration for the Millennium on the school playing field in 2000. This was open to all the village and offered the opportunity for a picnic together, providing some games and entertainment and the chance for local organisations to set up stalls and advertise their existence.

The results of the Millennium project researching the 'Derivation of the Street Names in the Parish of Staplehurst', which was also their idea, undertaken mainly because so many were obviously named after village people, were also first displayed on a forest of posts on the field at that celebration. It was fascinating to see who the people were and also to discover that there were still trust funds in place which offered grants to young people to kick start their careers. This work has since been issued in book form with later updates covering the newer estates. The Debt Club was also initially set up under the auspices of The Churches Together in Staplehurst and The Free Church now hosts the Parish food bank post COVID.

Obviously, there are, or were, several very active groups like the Horticultural Society, the Photographic Society, the Dramatic Society etc., all of whom demonstrate their skills at various exhibitions and performances which I have very much enjoyed and offer excellent outlets for furthering your hobbies and learning new ones. The WI, Men's Shed, Youth Club and Friends of All Saints are some other organisations with which you can get involved. The last of these is a charity set up in the 1990's with the sole aim of raising money to help with the upkeep of the fabric of All Saints Church which obviously, given its age and size, is very costly. This they do with member subscription and through various fund-raising events which include the annual Brain Game, and, up until Covid, the Shepherd's Market.

Then there are people who open their homes and gardens for garden safaris or give barbeques or dinners for charity. Auctions of Promises are also great fun whilst providing another valuable source of funding thanks to the goodwill of those offering their services. I have benefited from these myself including having my will written, having dinner prepared in my own home for up to 8 people and also learning how to do a barbeque successfully.

It goes without saying that Beavers, Cubs, Brownies, Scouts and Guides are all hugely important groups for youngsters and that they take up a great amount of time from very dedicated and committed people. The Monarchs Football Club also provides an equally valuable and welcome opportunity for all ages.

The commitment of so many people is awe inspiring and non more so than those who commit to deliver the Thursday Lunch Club, the monthly Sunday Lunches and the Weald Club for the Disabled weekly get-togethers, all of which take place in the McCabe Centre. They give such pleasure to so many people, not least in the opportunity to meet and chat. The weekly Interest Group is similarly a very time-consuming commitment for those who organise it and it serves up very enjoyable and diverse entertainment; again something for all interests.

The villagers' response to the difficulties caused by the COVID Pandemic was similarly impressive with the Parish Council leading the way by organising a call centre, volunteer network and food bank. Frankies Farm Shop also deserves a mention for changing its café into a shop and offering click and collect meals or home delivery.

Obviously, there is much more besides in the village which I have not touched on and probably even more of which I am ignorant, but this is only meant as a taster and furthermore, of this I am sure, Staplehurst offers something for everyone and it will always be there for anyone who is in need. You only have to ask.

My final accolade: A huge thank you for Good Friends and Good Neighbours!

A Poetry Competition

Malcolm Buller

In 1979 the Staplehurst Society organised poetry writing competitions for three age groups and the winning entries have been preserved in the society's archives. Mr Len Pettit and Mrs N Stoll were awarded cash prizes in the over 16 age group; Alison, Jason and Matthew in the 11 to 16s whilst Meg, Heidi and David won in the under 11s.

The theme was 'Staplehurst past, present and future' and nearly ninety entries were judged by Bert Seth. Mavis Chapman and Peter Day, Dramatic Society members, joined Bert Seth in reading the prize-winning entries at the presentation evening in the Parish Room. Would the same theme evoke similar responses 45 years later? There are many parallels.

A POETRY COMPETITION

David Bunting (10)

A Staplehurst man from Hong Kong
Let off a giant stink bomb
Five ladies cried
Six babies died
And the rest said, "Corr, what a pong!"

Jason Cannings (12)

Staplehurst, a lovely village
Free from looting, rape and pillage
The Roman road runs straight and true
Between the houses old and new

    The church is old and very grand
    It was carefully built and planned
    In the tower the bells ring loud
    To summon the faithful Sunday crowd

In the village and around
Society members do abound
They sometimes visit a stately home
Or frolic in a pond that is overgrown

    Londoners come down every year
    To pick the hops and drink the beer
    Staggering and shouting round the village,
    "Come back looting, rape and pillage!"

A POETRY COMPETITION

Heidi Gain (9)

Staplehurst used to be full of trees
    Lots of trees and lots and lots of leaves

Then the machinery came along
    It went, 'Drrr, buzz, hammer, hammer, dong!'

Now it's full of houses and flats
    Out of some houses come screeching cats.

Meg Fann (9)

It's a job to keep it tidy
'Cos it's dirty all the time
People go out to collect the litter
They start about nine.

    It's quite a noisy village
    With traffic zooming past
    Some people crash near our house
    'Cos they go so very fast.

There is a village library
Which is really very good
Where Teresa, Francis, Anne,
Will always help you if they can.

    Shops there are in plenty
    Garages, builders too
    A Chinese and a Chippy
    And a brand new public loo.

A POETRY COMPETITION

Alison Hegarty (15)

I know when I see the red brick
Stomachs of the oast houses
And see the valley carpets laid
Before me.

    I know when I walk by the railway line
    To pick blackberries or stand on the bridge
    To watch the rabbits leaping in the sunlight
    Or ride down Craddocks Lane on frosty evenings
    And smell the dusky sweetness of the Autumn.

I know when I wake to joyful church bells
Or the singing of the line to
the Dover train.

    And what do I know that these travellers
    Passing through another stop,

Along the line, do not?
Do they see friendly welcoming names
Of farms; here for posterity?
Aydhurst, Pagehurst, Spilshill, Chittenden.
Stand in time, not to be obscured.

    Do they retain the memories
    Of a school; where learning
    Was enjoyed?
    The school that never seems to forget
    The faces that it sees.

A POETRY COMPETITION

They only see the maze of little roads
As in their towns.
But these are named for –
Bathurst, Newlyn, Usborne, Reeves.

>They only hear the thundering lorries
>Storming through, as in their towns.
>But Loddenden remembers horse and carts;
>Carriages waiting at the Crown.

They don't know, that when after all the change
There'll ever be in Staplehurst
I'll live in and still hold affection for this place
Which always will be home to me.

Matthew Ralph (13)

The village postman's name is Jim,
Happy and helpful, that is him.
He delivers post to us every day.
Whistling cheerfully on his way.

>He turns his hand to everything,
>The old and lonely rely on him.
>A garden to plant and flowers to tend,
>A hole to dig, a fuse to mend.

Life in Staplehurst would be very thin
If it wasn't for the likes of postman Jim.

Poetry Group

Malcolm Buller

The Staplehurst Library User Group was formed in 2005 as part of a county initiative to foster greater involvement in local libraries. Just nine were set up. This small group helped our librarians, especially during the refurbishment, and arranged events with evening talks and poetry readings. After the Covid lockdown SLUG reformed and found that previous opportunities no longer existed. The emphasis was on forming self-running groups with minimal staff involvement. There are groups to suit all ages and interests so ask our friendly librarians about them.

In early 2023, emerged Staplehurst Library Poetry Group, meeting at 2pm for an hour on the last Wednesday afternoon of each month. Those present discuss the chosen theme and share what they have discovered. Reluctant at first, but having established trust amongst themselves, all have turned their hands to writing. One suggested theme, remembered from early school days, was 'Acrostic Poetry'.

Poetry

Perhaps words are mightier than the sword
Out of the heat of battle
Expectations can exceed reality
Trying to gloss over matt
Responding to wishes rather than needs
Your sharp – but truthful thoughts – have strength

Woodcutter

Sue Terry

Sue was inspired by the challenge of writing an Acrostic poem. Her thoughts turned to her quiet grandfather who worked in solitude in woodlands near Brenchley and Matfield. His family's children loved to roam and play there, having adventures, building rafts to float on the ponds, but also finding grandfather to wonder at his art.

Working away at his solitary task,
Overhead a cloudless blue sky,
On his knee, resting on a leather apron, his spokeshave ready to be used.
Dangling on a wire, his billy-can – tea gently simmering on a tripod over the fire
Chopping and shaping the chestnut poles – curly wood-shavings falling like small waves around his feet
Under the cool tarpaulin canopy lay his bread and cheese, wrapped in a cloth,
Tobacco in his waistcoat pocket hanging on a wood-stump,
The sounds of chopping and rasping echoing through the silent woods
Everywhere – surrounding the clearing – tall straight trees, waiting like sentinels
Relishing his lunch, the warm sun on his back, content in his solitude, enjoying the silence, broken only by the soft buzzing of a solitary bee amongst the bluebells.

Is That Funny?

Anita Thompson

Our tennis pro's a master of the game –
Gets results from all our kids to justify his fame.

But when he crashed the net –
And followed the ball – heels over tête –
Stood up – with bloody nose and teeth upset –
Stumped off court as umpire called out "Let!"

We all laughed like drains –
Anything that entertains!

It wouldn't have mattered on grass –
But asphalt is harsh.

He looked just like a battered kid.

Sorry Sid.

In 1967, the Coventry College of Education's Men's League Tennis Team was half-comprised of two long-term residents of Staplehurst. Can you identify them?

First Love

Moira Henderson

I was sixteen and never been kissed,
But at Ann's party, oh what bliss!

I'd met a boy, heart a flutter,
Looked like he wouldn't melt butter.

First date, off to the 'pictures', very dark,
Worried my make-up was too stark.

He tried to kiss me, "No! No! No!
I'm doing my GCE's you know."

I said goodbye - till the end of June.
He said I'd dumped him far too soon.

Founder's Day, scanning the place,
My friend Kath had scented lace

Afterwards we all filed out,
Spotting him, "Exams over!" I shout.
He said, "I'll see you about."

Out Of The Window

Anita Thompson

Our Aga cooker left today – in pieces –
Its skeleton lies on the path – in bits.
We bought it second-hand in 1960,
Erected it, bought coke and kettle that fits.
It warmed the kitchen well, dried all our clothes
and cooked like Mother did, as she admits.
Saved winter piglets' lives in the warming oven
when snow and large litters combined to freeze mum's tits,
but we faced every summer without it,
reduced to electrics for toast, jam and spits.
There's no coal now for domestic use
and anthracite's saved for steam trains and ships.
We've decided on oil central heating,
bought a second-hand Stanley – in bits.

Why Staplehurst?

Interest Group Members

One Friday morning in April 2024, Interest Group Members were invited to share the reasons for their coming to Staplehurst. They were recorded and the scripts edited to the stories below. There are similarities of course.

June Moore

I'm here because I was born here, as were my family for many generations past (LL-SS p2). Oliver Young and Emma Wood had fourteen children, which included two sets of twins (although sadly one of each pair died). My Gran and these Great-Aunts and Uncles all worked locally. My work was in Maidstone and Staplehurst was handy for my husband to take the train to London so I've never lived anywhere else. It's a very different village now, but I wouldn't want to move. I like the people.

Margaret Cramp

Both my parents were born in Maidstone and after they married, in 1922 they came to Staplehurst. I'm the youngest of the five children. (LL-SS p123). At eighteen I went away to college and then lived in London, Leeds Yorkshire, Edinburgh, and then Africa for nine years. I came back to Staplehurst because my family were here, including two of my sisters. There didn't seem any point in moving anywhere else. I was divorced and in time, married John Cramp whose maternal great-grandfather had bought a plot of land and built the house where John was born and where I still live. John and I were of similar ages and had always known each other. Eighty years ago, everyone knew everyone and the village was self-sufficient. Despite it having grown, I think and hope there is still a heart in our village where people care and look out for each other.

Susie Marklew

When I married in 1967, we lived in a flat above a launderette in South West Norwood. My grandparents had moved from the East End to Bathurst Road a couple of years earlier and when they saw where I was living, they gave me £200 for a deposit on a new bungalow in Iden Crescent. I moved to number 14 on the 14th June 1968. The following year my husband and I went to a dance in the Village Hall with some of our new neighbours. The four musicians in the band were not young rockstars! Unbeknown to us, our husbands had entered us into the competition the organisers were holding to find this year's 'Miss Staplehurst'. It was quite a shock, but we paraded round the hall with the other contestants. There were about twenty-five of us and my friend came in third place. Second went to a girl from St Mary's Convent, but to my surprise, I was declared the winner.

I was presented with a trophy and a prize of five pounds, which was a large amount considering that my monthly season ticket to London was eleven. Photographs were taken and later I was interviewed by Sylvia Lade who was the village correspondent for the Kent Messenger.

The Village Fete and Carnival (LL-SS p63) was amazing. A pretty float was created especially for us three girls, with a swing for me to sit on. However, we had to make our own dresses and I wanted to wear a long one, but that was not allowed. I had to be in white broderie anglaise which was very short. We processed all the way from the Station along the crowd-filled main road, through the estate to the Surrenden Field. It was a very sunny day and my Mum and very frail Dad travelled down from London, along with my brother, his now wife, her parents and brother to watch me make a short speech before declaring the fete open. Wearing my sash and crown, I was presented with a bunch of flowers and had a very happy day as the Carnival Queen.

WHY STAPLEHURST?

Maureen Brice

In 1975 my husband Ted and I came down from London to Tunbridge Wells to be tenant-landlords of a public house there. This means that one's accommodation is tied to the property, so thinking ahead to retirement, we decided to buy a house in advance. At that time my mother and sister Beryl were living in an area of London where there were many burglaries and a murder, so Beryl, Ted and I decided to join together for the purchase. The only place in the area where we could afford to buy was Staplehurst and we bought a small terraced house in Knowles Walk.

In 1980 Beryl and Mum moved in. We were not due to retire until 1989 but when the time came, Mum was still with us so there was no room for Ted and me in a small, two-bedroom terraced house. For a year we camped out with Beryl's very good friend, Anne Rivers, until we could move to a larger property in Oliver Road where I still live today. I won't ever move from such a wonderful and friendly village. In fact, I have lived in Staplehurst longer than anywhere else, so it really is home!

Bob Ham

Wendy and I were living up in Cumbria where I had gone to work. Wendy came from a very small village called Aspatria between Carlisle and Workington whereas Tonbridge was my home town. When my job came south, we became the last people to move into the new houses in Slaney Road. As we were putting down our deposit the agent had a phone call to say that the price had gone up £250 to £18,000, but he said it couldn't because he'd just sold it. That was in 1977 and in 1981 we almost moved away because I'd changed employer and the new firm asked me to move nearer their offices in Croydon. They offered us a bridging

WHY STAPLEHURST?

loan and we chose a house in Tonbridge which met their criteria, but when they saw that we were planning to move from one TN postcode to another, I was told we didn't have to sell up. Later the strip of land behind all of the houses in our road was offered for sale to residents so we enjoy a clear view over the designated Low Weald which has been important in fighting against development in the landscape.

Elsie Baum

While working as a sister for Leonard Cheshire in Mote House, Maidstone, it was decided to relocate the home to Staplehurst in 1995. I was asked to take an early holiday in June so that I could help move the residents on my return. I decided to go on a tour of India and in Delhi I met Alan who was also on the tour. We got on really well and decided to meet up in London on our return. It soon became clear that we wanted to be together and we chose Staplehurst where I now worked and Alan could commute to Hendon. After work, I visited Wards who said they had a small cottage in Chapel Lane. We got married in 1996 on the same day that Mote (Sobell) Lodge officially opened (LL-SS p69).

WHY STAPLEHURST?

Alan Baum

I worked as a lecturer at Middlesex University Business School in Hendon. I had been divorced for five years and asked colleagues at my Rotary Club to suggest an exotic place to go on holiday. Many of them were well travelled and suggested India. There were fifteen of us on the holiday and I was pleased to get on well with Elsie who was also on the trip. We decided to meet up again in London and Kent on our return. I was keen to get out of the capital and Staplehurst's direct line to Charing Cross and Northern Line to Hendon made it very suitable. We moved into a cottage in Chapel Lane on 15th December 1995. As the journey proved to be quite onerous, I decided to take advantage of an early retirement package the following year. We got married at the Archbishop's Palace in Maidstone on 1st October and I retired four days later. I did return for some part-time work as well as volunteering at Mote Lodge and at the Marden Heritage Centre.

Dorothy Crooks

We lived in a small village of grey-stone houses, five miles, uphill, from Leeds in Yorkshire. With moors surrounding us and a crossroads in the middle, it had many similarities to Staplehurst as people were mainly through-travellers. Even the old school buildings were very similar. The Pope and Hayward fizzy drinks company was matched by Drighlington's. As the new school was built up on the Civil War site of the Battle of Adwalton Moor, they kept digging up cannon balls and other artefacts. Standing outside, waiting for the children, was bleak as winter seemed to last from July to the end of May.

My husband's work transferred down here and it was a terrible shock. It was so much warmer! I stayed to sell our house whilst my husband worked and searched for a property. I brought the children down for a fortnight's holiday, but all we did was look at houses. House prices were double and it got to the final Friday when we went into an agent in Hawkhurst who knew of an empty house in Clapper Lane, Staplehurst, but the owner didn't live there. She rang and the phone was answered so we could view. It had an acre of land and was large so we needed a whopping-great loan to move in in 1975. We couldn't afford it really, but it was very nice. The garden attracted a wide range of wildlife like birds, rabbits and howling foxes in the pitch-black darkness. We had a young French exchange-student, Graziella, stay with us and she was miserable and terrified for the whole fortnight. She wouldn't speak to us in French or English, didn't want to eat (except for my puddings) or go anywhere. We found out later that she hadn't wanted to come away from her home in a bright, city, high-rise flat. What really spooked her was the owl hooting, every time the bathroom light was switched on.

We were very happy and both daughters were married from there, but one day my husband came in from cutting the grass and said he didn't want to do it anymore so, after twenty-one years, we moved to a bungalow in Hurst Close. Being able to walk to the village to join in activities was a great blessing rather than relying on my husband as chauffeur. I really feel that Staplehurst people look out for each other and I don't want to be anywhere else.

Malcolm Buller

Our families lived in the Eltham and Surbiton areas, but the early 70s house price inflation had forced us to move to Burton Latimer near Kettering in Northamptonshire where our two sons were born. We knew that if we were to move back south to be nearer family we had to do so before the boys were of school age. I started applying for teaching posts in Kent and was appointed to Headcorn Primary School in the winter of 1977. We wrote to local estate agents and, as soon as term finished for Christmas, we travelled to Eltham where Joan stayed with the boys whilst I drove over 200 miles to visit every agency I could find within an approximate ten-mile radius of the school. Maidstone, Ashford and all villages in between brought me to a place called Staplehurst where I found Douglas Maloney's on the corner of Fishers Road and Station Road. Two other agents at the other end of the village also had the same property on their books.

The next day Joan and I left the boys with their grandma, young aunt and uncle, and set off to visit the places and few properties we had chosen as possible from the scarce pickings. A box with few windows and a postage stamp garden, a semi in the rural landscape beside the A20 (before the M20 was built), a rambling rectory at Tovil and a semi a long way out of Headcorn village for Joan to push the pram, were all discounted without viewing inside. That left the Victorian, end-terraced house in the Marden Road, Staplehurst that, we discovered later, had been on the market for two years as no-one would buy it from the Irish builder. We paid nearly £16,000 and moved in on March 31st 1978, David's first birthday.

Shopping

Malcolm Buller

In the book 'Listening Lines – Staplehurst Stories' several authors wrote about the self-sufficiency of village life as everything possible was bought locally. There were many small shops and Jull's Emporium which seemed to offer almost everything (LL-SS p34). Dorothy Burgess's walk in the 1930s (LL-SS p99) and Trevor Jenkins's in the 70s (LL-SS p164) give many specific names of shopkeepers and Rory Silkin was delighted that there were four sweet shops between the church and butchers (LL-SS p206).

SHOPPING

The Staplehurst Dramatic Society programme in 1971 for 'The Taxpayers Waltz' cost 25p and doubled as the entrance ticket. Inside were advertisements which show what was offered by many of the local traders that served our village.

Hamilton & Co, Chartered Surveyors and Estate Agents, High St
Jeff Kinna, Furniture & Toys, Tall Tree Showroom, Station Rd (LL-SS p 95)
Diagrit Electrometallics Ltd
K & D Coltman, Groceries, greengroceries, ice cream, gents' hairdresser
Berners Hill Garage Ltd, for Simca and Lancia, Cranbrook Rd
The Bell Hotel (under new management)
Bretts Outfitters, footwear, school uniforms, dry cleaning, Church Hill
Lambert & Symes, Chartered Surveyors, Auctioneers, Estate Agents, High Street

SHOPPING

Homeleigh Timber Supplies, all D-I-Y requirements, Station Rd (LL-SS p227)
E.W. & G Wood, Fruiterers, greengrocers & florists, High St
Dixons Stores, grocer, off-licence and delicatessen, High St
Goblins Bookshop, (your new bookshop), High St
Kaydee, Latest London fashions
David O'Brien, Building, decorating and repairs, Marden Rd
R Chainey, Staplehurst Radio
Staplehurst Service Station, Texaco petrols, car products, High St
Diagrit Diamond Tools
C & E Gray, Tobacco, confectionery, toys, High St
Peter Chardry, Swimming pools, Little Craddock
A Boorman, family butcher, High St
The Weald Pharmacy, High St
The Venture Boutique, pottery, jewellery, paintings, antiques, rear of King's Head, Bell Lane
George & Martin, Building Contractors
A E Harmer, Grocer and draper, Crampton House, High St
Lampard Ltd, Vauxhall cars, Bedford vans, (**** petrol 34p per gallon), Station Rd (LL-SS p165)
Carpet Flair, (for Dramatic décor) High St

In 1999 a developer sent draft plans to the Parish Council, wishing to hold a meeting with them to discuss the possibility of building a supermarket to the west of the Railway Station. It was rumoured that it would be a Safeway store. A few years later, Tesco made a presentation to a Parish Council meeting about their plans to build a supermarket on the Railway Station car park, having made a leaflet drop through many doors. The leaflet contained many factual errors and the highly-paid representatives were woefully ignorant of this village. Instead of being welcomed with open arms as they expected, they received many comments and questions that they couldn't answer. The plan included moving the car park on to the northern side of the railway line with a single entrance and exit towards the east in George Street and placing a petrol station on the corner of the Maidstone Road and Station Approach. A full planning application was submitted to Maidstone Borough Council and then withdrawn.

In 2011 Sainsbury's put out a leaflet to residents and held a consultation event. This was followed in 2012 when a plan was submitted to build a supermarket on the factory side of Station Approach in cooperation with D.K. Holdings. Very quickly, Tesco re-submitted their plans. Village opinion was divided, but mainly favoured the Sainsbury's application. The leaflet offered a state-of-the-art factory building for D.K. Holdings, 150 jobs for local people, 171 parking places and included the provision of a free bus service to the store for up to three days per week for local residents. The Parish Council were in favour of the development, but asked that the bus stop outside be set back away from the roundabout beside a lay-by. In March 2013 the MBC Planning Committee Chairman decided that both applications must be heard in tandem, a procedure not experienced before. As the ward

SHOPPING

member for Staplehurst, the Chairman was clearly in favour of Tesco, but the Committee unanimously passed that of Sainsbury's with 27 conditions. After a split vote on the Tesco scheme, it was deferred. A short while later, a slightly altered scheme to reduce the impact of the new car park in George Street was refused. One small building was demolished on the new Sainsbury's site in 2016 to prove that work had started, but then, nothing else as all food companies stopped building new stores.

The Parish Council regularly asked Sainsbury's for updates on progress, but the responses were always non-committal. The Covid pandemic slowed things further. Finally, after demolition, pedestrian and traffic disruption, a skeleton building emerged in 2020. (The gas board severing the water main also didn't help.)

SHOPPING

Finally, on March 24th 2021, the store was officially opened. Shoppers queued to be welcomed into the store and many staff were on hand to help them find their way. Kent Online television interviewed some, including Cllr. Joan Buller who said that she looked forward to walking to the store each day and added that her husband was pleased not to have to drive her shopping anymore! Within weeks, the senior management had to agree that demand was far higher than they had predicted, the point made by the councillors on numerous occasions.

Fears had been expressed that a supermarket would destroy the businesses at The Parade which had been built in the style of many such places in the 1960s, but it was ram-raiding that hastened the demise of the last remaining bank. Commercial properties can change hands without local input so 'market forces' determine which business will be profitable and therefore which products are offered. Change is inevitable and so in 2024 we have many premises offering ready-prepared food, a betting shop and tattoo parlour.

SHOPPING

Despite the agreed condition, it was many months before an empty Hams minibus was seen arriving at Sainsbury's. Meetings were held with senior staff, councillors and myself to find out what was actually happening. Two rural routes had been devised, visiting Kilndown, Goudhurst, Cranbrook, Sissinghurst, Biddenden and Headcorn on a Tuesday whilst on Thursdays Marden and Curtisden Green were also involved. It was politely, but firmly pointed out that this was neither 'local' nor what had

SHOPPING

been signed off as the condition. (A copy of the signed Staplehurst Route was given to the staff.) The routes continued and investigation revealed that the only passengers were two from Marden occasionally. It took until March 2024 for the Staplehurst route to be implemented after I had travelled as a passenger with Robin, the very helpful driver. Three years of lost customers could now start to be recaptured, but the fear is that the service will not last.

Guiding in Staplehurst

Annette Holmes

My parents and I moved to Staplehurst in 1969 and when we were looking for a Guide Company for me to join, the nearest was in Marden. I joined and there I met Hilary Gower (nee Excell), along with June and Dawn Handly. Hilary's brother Alva, a Queen's Scout, would take us in his van. It was great fun and we would get chips and pickled onions, to which Alva would say, "Oh no. Not pickled onions. Yeuk!"

One week we were told that our Guide Captain was moving away and that her Seconder could not take over. That meant that the company would have to close. We were obviously all very upset by this, but we were told about a lady who had just moved into Staplehurst and that we should go to see her. Her name was Kathy Lamb; her husband was Barry and they had two boys; Gordon aged 4 and David 2.

Kathy agreed to start the 1st Staplehurst Guide Company with Maralyn and Judy Radford. We had so much fun. We did a lot of badge work which later enabled me to get the Queen's Badge, the highest award in Guides. We made camp fires, cooking pancakes on tin cans, singing songs, making gadgets. Camp was always fun and at one I was given a new name. While I was sent running around the field the others mixed powders and liquids in a bowl. Then they all ran out to catch me and when they had, they tied me to the flagpole. They covered me with their smelly mixture and named me 'Puffin'.

I remember us performing the play 'Snow White' and every year on 22nd February we had 'Thinking Day'. This date was the birthday of Lord and Lady Baden Powell. Each patrol chose a different country to research and we then cooked their food for us all to enjoy as we learnt about these different nations. We had flag competitions and all learnt how to hold and march with it. We learnt the signs when following trails, tracking and important first aid skills.

GUIDING IN STAPLEHURST

Guiding had grown in the village and we had the 2nd and 3rd companies. Kathy Lamb succeeded Freda Tomlin as Guide Commissioner and so my Mum, Joyce Dart, took over the 1st company. After I achieved my Queen's Award, I became a Young Leader and joined the Dolphin Rangers, run by Pat and Ken Morgan. We went on a trip to the Shropshire Canal where we enjoyed steering the boat, working the locks and taking turns to cook. When I was 21, I gained my camp licence. I started up the 4th Staplehurst Company with helpers Linda Savage and Pat Dallman. (Both of their daughters gained the Queen's Award.) We had so much fun helping the girls enjoy flower arranging, making Christmas cards, table decorations, star gazing, map reading, working for many badges and so much more. We also had tent pitching competitions with other guide companies and enjoyed beating the scouts! Yo!

GUIDING IN STAPLEHURST

The ex-guides can join Trefoil, meeting in the Kathy Lamb Guide Centre, where we enjoy many different activities, go on walks and have interesting talks. One recently was about Hypo Hounds where dogs are trained to alert diabetic patients of a change in their blood sugars. We were told of a dog in the home being agitated and the mother alerted the school staff who found the son's levels were critically low. Another charity talk, by Making Miracles, was about a knitting scheme where garments are sold to raise funds for counselling for mothers who have lost babies. Support is also given to the Guide Dog charity and the Buttercup Goat Sanctuary. We adult members can still work towards gaining badges as our group is doing, working together for our 'Motivate' badge, raising money for the vital work of the Air Ambulance. Individually I am using my recent cruise to help gain the 'Voyage' award. Guiding lasts a lifetime!

A Token Of Staplehurst

Malcolm Buller

The following is based on a copy of an article by Richard H Hardy in 'Bygone Kent' which is housed in the Staplehurst Society's archives.

Especially in poorer rural areas of England in some periods of the 17th, 18th and 19th centuries, coins were in short supply. George III objected to his head being shown on such a base metal as copper and parliamentarians saw little need for them. The machinery for minting was outdated and the process too expensive to bother with low-value coinage. The solution was for traders to strike their own tokens and give these as change, thus also ensuring that customers would return to make more purchases. From 1648 to 1672, tokens were small and crudely made, usually with just the issuer's initials and the year shown. 103 towns and villages in Kent are known to have had such tokens in circulation.

With the industrial revolution came the power to produce supplies from the Welsh copper mines in sufficient quantity to be able to produce many copper penny tokens. 23 villages in Kent produced tokens in the last decade of the 18th century, of which Staplehurst was one, issued by John Simmons, a gentleman farmer. The halfpenny shows the crest of a stag's head and the initials I S in script. (Capital J was shown as I in that era.) On the reverse is the Kent horse and the legend 'FOR CHANGE NOT FRAUD'.

Cricket In Staplehurst

A Cricketer

There is good reason to believe that cricket has been played in and around Staplehurst for over 250 years. For most of that time a Staplehurst Cricket Club, or an organisation that was recognisable as such, has been in existence. The earliest reference to the game here comes from the 'Kentish Weekly Post' of 9th July 1743 where Horsmonden had beaten a team from Romney, Cranbrook and Staplehurst and that a return match was to be played two days later. In 1799, another report said that on Whit Wednesday, Wateringbury would be hosting Staplehurst.

In 1819 on August 3rd, the 'Maidstone Journal' reported that Staplehurst's 66-year-old Mr Stephen Thwaites and his ten sons, aged 30 to 11, had beaten a Headcorn team. Shortly afterwards, in a history of the county game in Kent by R.L. Arrowsmith, he described the evils of heavy betting that was affecting the game. It was probably in the early 1820s that Sutton Valence earned £100 for beating Staplehurst, which was a considerable sum in those days and it broke the club. (The winning team was coached by John Willes who is credited by some with introducing the round-arm style of bowling. Born in Headcorn, it is said that he asked his sister to help him practise his batting, but as her crinoline got in the way, she bowled over-arm to him. Realising the potential, he used it in a Kent match, but being no-balled, he stormed out of the ground. Perhaps that is why he earnt his money another way.) The club was back in action by 1823 and reports appeared in newspapers regularly through the decades. A tombstone in the All Saints' Churchyard is inscribed, 'This stone is erected by the Staplehurst Cricket Club as a mark of respect to the memory of Edwin Fitch, who died January 22nd 1869, aged 43 years'.

Research in the archives of the 'Maidstone Journal', 'Kent Messenger' and 'Village Notes' brings to life the matches played, largely through the printing of scorecards. Many matches were against the local villages, but other teams are no longer in action. The Curate, Dr Highwood and Rev. Thomas Thatcher feature regularly along with the Offen, Austen, Bright and Wickings families, as well as many individuals. Scores were much lower than today's totals, probably due to the less-true surfaces, and quite often each team had two innings. In August 1907, J Midgley, playing against Frittenden, took hat-tricks in both innings.

Exactly where matches were played is harder to locate and date. The Tithe map of 1842 shows the field numbered 962 as 'Cricket Field' in its index and its usage being 'pasture'. This was to the west of 'Sawpit Field' which bordered the Cranbrook Road at its junction with the Frittenden Road. How long the field had been called 'Cricket' is unknown, but as announcements in papers for the early parts of that century mention that cricket meals would be provided in the Crown, it seems most likely that this was the team's home venue under what is now Iden Crescent, Hanmer Way and beyond.

At the end of the nineteenth century, reports start to refer to matches being played at Iden Park. On 4th May 1895, the Kent Messenger reported that 'the Iden Rovers matches are rapidly drawing to a close, but the ground in Iden Park so generously placed at the disposal of the club by Mr W Hoare, will shortly be utilised for cricket and practice games will be commenced almost immediately'. The Iden Manor Cricket Club played occasional matches and represented Iden Manor Estate in 'Cricket Weeks', run by the estate and elsewhere. (A large box with the initials I.M.C.C. is kept in the pavilion.) Other contemporary reports are of a Staplehurst Cricket Club playing at the same time. Also, the Frittenden Road ground was used (after hay-making), but which team played where is open to debate. Bill Tipples Senior thought the Staplehurst Club played at Iden Park and I.M.C.C. at the Frittenden Road ground, but by 1911, Henry Veall's evidence shows the Staplehurst Club playing at the Frittenden ground and there are no further reports on the I.M.C.C. This team probably disbanded around the sale of the Iden Manor Estate in 1904. William Hoare was a very keen cricketer and the Kent C.C. President in 1900, but the new German owner, D.A. Seligman, was not. It is natural to suppose that this saw an amalgamation take place. In 1907 plans were drawn up for a pavilion to be built and A. Seligman first appeared on a scorecard. Bert Thirkell (SS-LL p13) said that this was Arthur who had a brother, David. He may have been the owner, or they were his sons. The construction was not completed until 1914 (Sid Austen was one of the builders) and Frank Bourne thought the opening was rushed to August because of the onset of the first World War.

Minutes and score books, fixture lists and other documents have been retained since the war and it is clear that the leadership of J.W. Hewitt as captain produced a very exclusive club. Exceptional ability was needed for any local to make the team and it is said that residents who arrived to watch would recognise no-one and have to ask which team were batting. It was at this time that a corner of land was set aside for lawn tennis. This helped to normalise the club in the 1930s and, either side of the second World War, Staplehurst's club could be considered typical of a village; playing regularly and financing its activities with raffles, jumble sales and dances. In 1950 the Warmsley family donated the field to the club and this allowed the expansion of numbers of teams and the pavilion. The growing reputation of the club brought testimonial matches for Kent cricketers to the ground. The inclusion of juniors in coaching and games has helped support every aspect of the development into the Staplehurst Cricket and Tennis Club of the twenty-first century.

My Adventures

Chris Sharp

My story begins with Queen Victoria who was not amused when my great-great-grandfather made comments about Prince Albert. Thomas Crick was the Rector of Little Thurlow, Suffolk, who stated that the German Prince should not be made Chancellor

of the University of Cambridge. Outraged, the Queen banished Thomas to the wilds of Kent to a village called Staplehurst in 1846. With his wife Francis Katherine, he had three sons and three daughters. Of these, one was Alice Mary who married Benjamin Sharp in 1885. They had three sons, one of whom was my grandfather, Percival Maurice Sharp, and two daughters. Thomas worked hard as Rector of Staplehurst until his death in 1876. He was buried back in his first parish.

I have lived in Staplehurst in the same house, Swiss Cottage, for over fifty years so I have seen a lot of changes. When my parents moved here in 1958 there was no Chestnut Avenue or Corner Farm estate. Previous owners named the chalet Swiss Cottage because it reminded them of their holiday home. I have one brother who lives in Somerset and he occasionally comes back to visit me. Living on my own has its challenges, but I do alright.

MY ADVENTURES

I went to school at Dulwich Prep and Bethany. I used to help the milkman on his rounds which I enjoyed. I still visit customers with their Avon orders. I have helped for many years with the Parish Clean-ups and collect door-to-door for the Royal British Legions Poppy Appeals.

In 1926 my mother's father, Richard George Harvey Lowe, took a hat-trick at Lords when his bowling helped Cambridge beat Oxford. I have the ball with its engraved band that he was allowed to keep. He also played for Kent. It is no wonder that I have always had a keen interest in cricket. This led me to visit Staplehurst's ground in the Frittenden Road where I offered to become the scorer. For many people, keeping score is difficult, but I enjoy using pencil to note every ball in the over, every run to each batsman or extras and how each bowler performs. At first this was done at the pavilion, but in the 1990s a purpose-built score box was erected with its pulley-controlled run indicators and shade from the fiercest summer sun. After our team had won the league, everyone gathered in the pavilion. Through the crowd came a uniformed lady who asked who was called Christopher.

Having been identified, she told me she was arresting me for not paying for my train ticket. I was worried, and even more embarrassed when it was revealed that she was a kissogram.

As a life-member of Kent Cricket Club I have visited the matches at Beckenham, The Neville ground in Tunbridge Wells, The Mote in Maidstone and well as Canterbury, but nowadays they prefer to keep costs down by not playing at the smaller grounds. I did follow the team to Edgbaston to see Kent win the 20-20 final.

Father's father, Percival, was a captain in the 10th Royal Fusiliers in the First World War. After a bullet passed through his arm it then killed his batman. Grandfather then fought in the Russian Revolution between the Whites and Reds before returning to work for Coutts Bank. Following that he was ordained and became a canon at Rochester Cathedral.

I do enjoy going on jaunts. I'm a member of the National Trust and English Heritage as I really like history. I've visited the memorials and war graves in France and travelled to the most northerly part of Britain, Muckle Flugga which is nearer to the North Pole than to London.

A Staplehurst Cricketer's Dream – Barbados

Colin Breed

I have a lot to thank Staplehurst Cricket and Tennis Club for. This gem of a club is tucked away in the south of the village off the Frittenden Road, overlooked by the lovely Grade 1 listed, All Saints Church, the oldest building in the village.

A STAPLEHURST CRICKETER'S DREAM

Back in the early summer of 1992 when I was nearing the end of a long career in the Kent Police, (LL-SS p113) I was approached by a sadly now-departed friend and work colleague, Chris Longfield. He played cricket for Staplehurst and he cajoled me into playing a couple of games for them. Cricket had always been my great sporting love, but a few years earlier, because of my personal circumstances and heavy workload, I had given up playing. At the time I was living on my own in a police house behind the headquarters in Sutton Road, Maidstone. One game for Staplehurst was enough for me to fall back in love with the sport and to join the club. The friendly people, the lovely ground and the vibrant village in the heart of the beautiful Kent countryside; what was there to dislike? I determined then that on retirement I was going to move to Staplehurst.

A STAPLEHURST CRICKETER'S DREAM

In June 1996 I bought a house within walking distance of the club, ensuring that socialising in the bar was not a problem! Earlier in the year, I had met Val who, at the time, lived in Maidstone and also worked at police headquarters. By an amazing coincidence, Val had had a long association with Staplehurst, having been born in one of the cottages at Cross-at-Hand. She was brought up in the area and her mother was living in the village. It all fell together neatly in 2000 when we married in All Saints Church.

Thanks to Chris Longfield and Staplehurst Cricket and Tennis Club, cricket was well and truly back in my life. Little did I know back in 1992 of the experiences they would open up for me at an age when many players were hanging up their boots. In 1996 I was invited to play for Kent Over 50's in the national county championship, and a year later to join their squad for a tour to take part in the Barbados Over 50's Cricket Festival. I didn't need to think about it before accepting. The festival spanned two weeks and comprised of ten teams: five from the United Kingdom – Wales, Hertfordshire, Somerset/Wiltshire, Warwickshire/Hereford/Oxon and Kent, three from Barbados, one from Trinidad and Tobago and another from British Columbia. The late Len Morris who, for many years worked tirelessly for the expansion of seniors' cricket and was a stalwart of Horton Kirby Cricket Club, was our Kent Over 50's manager.

I travelled with my cousin, Keith Millen, who is like a brother to me and who also played cricket for Staplehurst for a number of years. For both of us this was the adventure of a lifetime as, until then, neither of us had travelled very far from home. We were well into our flight from Gatwick and I was marvelling at how we could fly at 30,000 feet for seven hours over one ocean and was generally getting childishly excited about what was to come when Keith suddenly exclaimed in an urgent voice, "Oh no." Being a little nervous, I looked out of the cabin window expecting to see something horrific such as an engine on fire. "What is it?" I asked with some trepidation. "I've left the washing out and it's raining. Alison will be furious when she gets home." A sign of things to come!

First impressions

Three things stick in my memory of our first hour in Barbados. The searing heat as we stepped onto the tarmac; the two porters each equally determined to carry my luggage through Customs for the obligatory dollar; and the frenetic fifteen-minute drive to the hotel. Those who have been to the West Indies will know what I mean when I say their bus and taxi drivers are something else! There were nine of our Kent party in a minibus with luggage jammed all around us. I could not believe that these pleasant, extremely laid-back Bajan people could be transformed into maniacal drivers. Our man seemed to aim at gaps in the narrow roads and then drove at breakneck speed, totally ignoring the many potholes, for fear the gap might suddenly disappear. It was only the luggage that was keeping us upright! That first Caribbean rum punch was certainly needed when we staggered exhausted into the hotel, much hotter than the 32 degree heat warranted.

Our Kent party stayed at the beautiful Cassuarina Beach Club, a four-star hotel set in seven acres of tropical gardens, alongside a long sandy beach at Christchurch on the south-west side of the island. It was a picture-postcard location with a palm tree lined beach and the crystal clear warm blue sea. Steel bands seemed to be obligatory in all the bars with twice daily "happy hours" enjoyed by us all around the pool. And to play cricket as well. Paradise indeed.

On the second evening the organisers laid on a buffet and drinks party for all the teams and supporters. Two famous West Indian cricketers, Sir Garfield Sobers and Sir Everton Weekes attended, both of whom had some fine tales to tell. The mistake the organisers made was allowing free drinks all evening with the first matches the next day. At 10pm I found my cousin Keith sprawled out asleep on the patio, head lolled back with his mouth wide open. Not a pretty sight.

Getting down to business

The next day, after consuming several doses of paracetamol, we played our first 35 overs-a-side match against the combined Somerset/Wiltshire team at a nearby ground. Scoring runs was not easy on the slow and low wicket which seemed to be made up of mud and grass cuttings baked hard in the extreme heat. It was easier to adapt to the bowling conditions and all our bowlers performed well, but we narrowly lost a low-scoring game.

Driving the point home

Next up for us was one of the Barbadian teams, played at the well-known Wanderers ground where England had played a warm up match on their last winter tour. Unfortunately, it had rained hard the previous night and again in the morning and the wicket was a sea of mud and grass cuttings. It looked unplayable. Our mini-bus driver didn't endear himself to the groundsman when he drove us onto the pitch and parked inside the boundary in front of the pavilion. When we had unloaded and he tried to drive off, mud flew everywhere and the back wheels sank into the soft grass! Instead of stopping he accelerated even harder, driving the wheels deeper. Some of us then had to push the vehicle out, leaving deep tyre tracks in the ground, hot and irritable players and an unimpressed groundsman. In England the ground would have been unfit for a week, but the typically laid-back groundsman shrugged his shoulders and told us that all he required was a rake, some grass cuttings to bond the mud, a roller, and sun to turn it all back into a shiny concrete-type finish! He added that we would be able to play in a couple of hours, which we did, and we wished we hadn't!

We eventually played a 25 overs-a-side game. I have never played in such conditions. The surface water had dried in the heat, but the bowlers' ends were still muddy. It was impossible and dangerous at our age to run in to bowl. In order to keep our feet, we had to bowl off a couple of paces. When we fielded first we soon realised why the opposition were so keen to play. They had secured as their opening batsman a certain George Braithwaite. He used to play for Barbados and was revered on the island. Yours truly helped him on his way when I dropped him early on in his innings. Thereafter, with clean hitting and embarrassing ease he scored 100 in 18 overs. In the first match I had bowled 7 overs for 16 runs. In this one, 5 overs for 47. Needless to say, we fell short of their 175 runs. The only consolation I had was some batting practice and a 'not out' score at the end.

Seeing the sights

Keith and I spent the weekend exploring the island by hiring a Mini Moke (which have no doors or windows and are great fun, that is if you have a padded backside as springs don't seem to be in their design). Now highly tanned, in our shorts and T-shirts, wearing the cricketers' shades and baseball caps round the wrong way, we bombed around the beautiful island thinking we were the cat's whiskers. The oldest swingers in town!

Out third match was at the excellent Barbados Bank ground and our opponents were the combined Warwickshire/Hereford/Oxon side. After a dreadful start batting first on a soft wicket, with the ball spinning prodigiously, we recovered and forged an unlikely win. Although we only scored a modest 140, by the time we fielded, the wicket had dried out and was by far the quickest we had played on. I relished bowling in these conditions and in my seven overs managed to remove three of their main batsmen, including to my delight, the middle stump of an ex-England and Sussex player, Alan Oakman. We ran out winners by 23 runs. We lost our fourth game against a strong Barbadian side by four wickets. Once again batting was difficult on a wicket where the surface had been baked hard by the sun, but underneath the ground was still soft from the heavy rain. The effect was like setting glue with the top surface moving slowly underfoot. It felt weird and none of us had experienced anything like this before. Batting seemed like a new art form.

The icing on the cake!

The final match of the tour was a grand affair in Bridgetown at the Kensington Oval, the Barbados test match ground, between an England and Wales X1 and a West Indies X1. I was lucky enough to be selected along with another Kent player, Mike Baldock. It was an honour to play on such a famous old ground where so many great cricketers had performed before. A close run 35 over match resulted with the West Indies overhauling our 187 in the last over of the game. Later, during the ceremony in the bar, I enjoyed talking to Alan Oakman and another great West Indian cricketer, the legendary fast bowler Wes Hall, about their time as professional cricketers.

And it all came to an end so quickly. Although Kent had only won one game and so didn't win the competition, the results didn't seem to matter. For a cricket lover it is difficult to imagine a better holiday. Plenty of sun, glorious beaches, wonderful scenery, endless "happy hours" with such friendly people and, of course, some serious cricket on lovely grounds. Heaven!

And it was all down to Staplehurst Cricket & Tennis Club

Without the encouragement of Chris Longfield and the friendly environment of the Club, I would not have returned to the game I love so much. In 1992 they opened up an amazing chain of events, which led to me playing cricket for over 30 more years (and counting) including representing Kent and England Senior sides, further cricket tours to Barbados and St. Lucia, marrying a local girl in All Saints Church in 2000, and forging new long-lasting friendships in both the superbly appointed clubhouse and in the village with its real community spirit.

Staplehurst – A Dramatic Society

Dorothy Crooks & Lorna Manning

After the Second World War, spirits were raised by the formation in 1946 of the Staplehurst Dramatic Society, under the leadership of Mrs Dora Lupe who had been involved in drama in Surrey. She felt this village could do with a comedy to help residents shake off the gloom with 'Lord Richard in the Pantry' and then 'A Quiet Weekend'.

Soon after Lorna and her husband Barrett (LL-SS p68) arrived in Staplehurst in 1964, she went to see a production because her neighbour, Maureen, was performing. 'The Brides of March' caused great controversy, reported in Local and National Press, and all three performances were sold out. As the Birmingham Rep were about to stage the same play, they wanted a block-booking, but there was no room. The reason for the fuss was that actresses would be wearing 'scanty costumes', but not a single complaint was received. The Society Chairman, John Gillett, said, "They were wearing more than some bikini-clad girls you see down at Hastings."

The Society was based in a hut at the rear of the Village Hall in Station Road. Crammed within these damp and musty walls were the props, wardrobe and scenery from past productions, ready to be re-cycled for the next. Similarly, any donation of clothing was readily accepted with the understanding that it might be severely altered before making a production appearance, as well as well-aired before wearing! The twice-weekly rehearsals focussed on learning the lines and movements whilst hammering and painting added to the chaos.

Dorothy and her husband, Bryn, arrived in 1975 and joined the Society where Lorna was an already established performer. In 1977 Lorna played the Cannibal Queen in 'Robinson Crusoe' and remembers that the King was a very small person from the junior group, in contrast to her very tall queen. The massive bone through the hair, huge jewellery and grass skirt were fine, but the brown greasepaint left its mark around the bath after all four performances. Lorna was pleased to travel home under the cover of darkness. Being tall in stature, Lorna was disappointed never to be given the romantic-lead roles, but did enjoy playing the glamorous lady in 'How the Other Half Loves' who was horrid to everyone. Miss Edith Burdett, who knew a lot about acting techniques and also made Shakespearean costumes from old velvet curtains, gave Lorna a very difficult part where she could not laugh or smile throughout the play, 'The Chalk Garden'.

The society members regularly built a float for the Carnival and Fete parade (LL-SS p63) based on their last or upcoming production. One year the rain was so heavy that members tore a hole in the side of the float and sheltered inside, certain that there would be no-one lining the streets who would notice their absence. After the long procession from the station along the High Street the floats reached the Surrenden Field where, dressed in their costumes, members would run to man their stalls. 'Fishing for Ducks' was very popular with the little children who always seemed surprised that they couldn't keep the duck, but were rewarded with a small prize instead.

STAPLEHURST – A DRAMATIC SOCIETY

In most years the Society put on two productions. The serious plays tackling works by eminent writers such as Alan Ayckbourn, Terence Rattigan and Oscar Wilde attracted smaller audiences whilst comedies proved ever-popular. Pantomimes made a profit. In 1969 'The Anniversary' was an appropriate choice, followed by 'The Chalk Garden'. In some years the two shows seemed to be linked, such as in 1978 'Mrs Warren's Profession' 'How the Other Half Loves', 1979's 'Ring Around the Moon' 'Sailor Beware' and in 1980, 'Pull the Other One' 'Humpty Dumpty'. The following year saw 'The Importance of Being Earnest' followed by 'Blithe Spirit' whilst 1982 had 'Watch it Sailor!' followed by 'Snow White and the Seven Dwarfs'. The efforts for 1983 are well remembered as, Jan Walker, a regular cast member, involved her son, now better known as Harry Hill, (LL-SS p28) to write the sketch show based on village characters and called 'Up Staplehurst!'. As well as a chaotic Parish Council meeting, action involved visits to the Rector (LL-SS p147), Homeleigh where Lill (LL-SS p227) would make up a price and the many adventures of Peter Day's bike (LL-SS p121).

Productions were in the Village Hall, but the staging was extended forwards to allow for greater movement. Other clubs had to forego their meetings as this and scenery were erected. The Society regularly entered the Three-Act Kent Drama Festival for which one of the visiting judges would write a critique and assess their performance. Usually about 30 plays were compared and standards were very high.

As well as the public performances, each year the members and their families attended the one-act evening for a social meal in the summer. Included were two or three short plays which gave experience amongst friends to fledgling actors, directors and occasionally writers. Lorna was anxious to produce a play which avoided using the usual drawing room set, so required just men (who were always in short supply) inside a coalmine. Davey lamps, cold tea and sandwiches were made and dirty costumes were easy. The atmosphere was tense after the cave-in, but when one man dried-up, Lorna lowered her pitch in an attempt to sound more masculine, but her prompt only engendered howls of laughter. She decided not to produce again.

Dorothy recalls how at the height of the River Dance fever, they rehearsed Irish Dancing and hinted that they would be having a guest appearance by a star celebrity. It wasn't Michael Flatley who pirouetted onto the stage in a tutu and bandana, but of course, Peter Day, who was always willing to play the fool. At a house-warming party, dressed in a nightie, he lay on a sun-lounger as Sleeping Beauty. Who dared wake him with a kiss? As President of the Society, Peter ran meetings his way which made some difficulties for Secretary Lorna, trying to take the minutes, but he always encouraged members to enjoy what they were doing, as did Bert Seth before him, although in a rather more subdued style.

Junior members were encouraged to join their own group which Dorothy organised. They came mainly from the families of existing members and as teenagers, put on some performances at the summer meal, but as with many such groups, exams and college saw numbers and commitment fluctuate. A one-act play taken from Victor Hugo's 'Les Miserables' involved a missing pair of candlesticks. A very nervous actor came on declaring that he had found them, only to realise that he had left them on the other side of the stage. Especially in pantomimes, there could be really small children involved as well as a lady in her nineties. One wife complained that after rehearsals her husband's jumper had strange lumpy indentations that she had to wash and iron out. He obviously hadn't owned up to playing the Dame. Dorothy did remind her that there were far worse things he could have been up to twice a week.

When Lorna was responsible for props a co-respondent's shoe was a vital part of the plot. It was a brogue, white and brown like a golf shoe, and was supposed to be casually discarded into an armchair. With too much enthusiasm behind it, the shoe bounced and disappeared into the front two rows of the audience! Lorna had until the next scene to find another shoe and smother it in appropriately coloured make-up or crawl into the audience to find her lost sole. On another occasion, when an actor suddenly jumped to several scenes ahead, he started talking about the magic lamp which Aladdin was yet to find, so Lorna as prompt, had to interrupt him boldly to wake him up and jolt him back a few pages.

Pantomimes were just that behind the scenes. With up to thirty participants, many with several different costumes and no dressing rooms available, changing took place anywhere, across the courtyard in the drama hut or in the courtyard itself and all with the winter winds reaching parts they shouldn't. There was no place for modesty.

When the old Village Hall reached the end of its time, the transfer to the old school was disastrous for the Dramatic Society. The loss of the hut meant that members tried to store props and costumes. Where could they rehearse without having to hire a room? The performances that were staged had to be built inside the totally unsuitable North Hall and space for the audience was limited. Sadly, after nearly seventy years, the Society had to fold.

Retirement Home

Malcolm Buller

The hoops that must be jumped through to gain permission to build are regularly moving, along with the goalposts. William the Conqueror limited the design of manor houses from purporting to be castles. Each change of monarch, and then parliament, has brought fresh, or stale, ideas. As layers of bureaucracy have increased, so have the numbers of documents and policies that must be considered. Inevitably within these, loopholes can be found and exploited.

RETIREMENT HOME

The build-up of vehicles in the twentieth century brought about a need for filling stations and garages. In the 1970s Lampard's at the corner of Station Approach offered fuel and Vauxhall cars, while Texaco at Sayner's near the crossroads in the High Street were both fondly remembered by Trevor Jenkins (LL-SS p164). Central Garage and the Forge were two more in the High Street. At the turn of the century, the Texaco garage had a small repair shop and a hire-car franchise. Permission was sought and gained to put housing on the site which was then boarded up. Anticipating the building of their supermarket, Sainsbury's bought the site and submitted plans to enlarge the number of pumps and stock a convenience shop. But then everything slowed down and stopped.

In 2021 Churchill Retirement Living submitted plans to Maidstone Borough Council to build on the garage site. These immediately caused alarm in the village as the scale of the development would bring it far further forward than the existing

RETIREMENT HOME

buildings and the parking provision for the anticipated number of residents was totally inadequate. The applicant's existing developments appeared to be in towns or village locations with excellent infrastructures. In its comments to the MBC Planning Committee, the Parish Council pointed out the inadequacy of parking for the residents of the 27 apartments and two cottages, along with staff and visitors, as well as the lack of any contributions to the infrastructure of the village. MBC refused the application, but an Inspector passed it on appeal.

After the demolition of the buildings, the removal of fuel tanks and sorting out the contaminated land from the garage, a huge crane was erected, but the Wealden clay slowed progress. The schedule of works showed the expectation that completion would be by June 2024, but by that date, the footings had barely been completed. How harmoniously will the finished site fit into the village and will any new residents be happy with Staplehurst's resources, along with the bus timetables? Only time will tell.

The Men's Shed

Richard James

Perhaps unexpectedly, our Men's Shed was instigated by a woman, Mira Martin.

The very first meeting was on 7th December 2016 when Mira was joined by Don Elliott. He was the only person to respond to the appeal for people to help set up a Shed by Mira, the Kent County Council Community Warden for Staplehurst. Don too thought it was such a brilliant scheme he wanted one here in the village. As soon as they were able to start using the Youth Club as a base, he set up some coffee mornings, with his friend Stan Twort in charge of making the refreshments.

On 23rd February 2017 the Shed started with only 6 members, but had help from a small council grant and support from KCC Councillor Eric Hotson and the Staplehurst Carnival and Fete Committee. Staplehurst Parish Council supported us and initially administered the funding until Bob Howse sorted out the banking arrangements for The Shed. Paul Kelly and the other trustees of the Youth Club agreed to allow the use of the hut without charge.

THE MEN'S SHED

Under the caption "Community gains as its men head back to the shed", the Kent Messenger published an article and picture showing Mira and Don with Alan Thomas, Bob Howse, Stan Twort and Colin De'ath.

Men's Sheds started in Australia to tackle the growing problem of isolation among the male population, arising from the idea that a stereotypical man potters about (and hides) in his shed. The idea was that Men's Sheds are similar to garden sheds – a place to pursue practical interests at leisure, to practise skills and enjoy making and mending. The difference is that garden sheds and their activities are often solitary in nature while Men's Sheds are the opposite. (My brother Tony who lives in Sydney, Australia told me – "I go there, pretend to make something while having a chat.") The scheme was introduced into Britain by Age UK in 2009. By early 2017 there were more than 300 Men's Sheds across the country. Many were focusing on woodwork and offering people a chance to learn and share valuable skills as well as to socialise.

While some Men's Sheds concentrate solely on the practical aspect, Staplehurst's is much more about the social side. For many of us, retirement is a massive change. Although it gives us lots of free time it can also mean fewer friends and for some, can lead to feelings of isolation and loneliness. Men typically find it more difficult to build social connections than women, and unlike women of a similar age, fewer older men have networks of friends and rarely share concerns about health and personal worries. There is more and more evidence that shows the negative impact of loneliness and isolation can be as hazardous to our health and wellbeing as obesity and excessive smoking. Surveys from mental health charities are finding that millions of people report feeling lonely on a daily basis.

As Mira Martin pointed out, "Men don't have the W.I. or the tea or coffee afternoons women have — it allows them to go away and have a chat." Don Elliott added, "I have never been lonely in my life, but there are a lot of lonely people about and if I can do anything to help even just one then I shall do it." The publicity of that newspaper article was very important in raising awareness and 8 current members joined shortly afterwards.

In July 2017, Nigel Sheeran joined the Shed. As a recently retired professional programme manager, he used his energy, enthusiasm and leadership skills towards building up the Staplehurst Men's Shed. A year later membership had grown from 7 to 25 and ours was awarded runner-up in the UK Men's Shed Association "Shed of the Year 2018" award. Nigel led the development of a wide range of activities, while retaining the original purpose to be a place where men can meet, have fun, socialise, feel safe and reduce the risks associated with isolation.

Nigel organised monthly speakers or focus days. These included talks from 'Kent Wildlife' to 'How to avoid be scammed in today's technological world'. Especially relevant was an event raising awareness of prostate cancer and raising funds for Prostate Cancer UK. That included a 'pub game marathon' at the cricket club which also saw the sponsored shaving of the normally very bearded John Wills and the walk by Alan Last and David Mackenzie in a rollator from Marden to Staplehurst. The emphasis on health led to the regular walks for members. Not only good exercise, but this was the opportunity for a good ramble, combining both meanings of the word. Some members attended first-aid courses and then held first-aid lessons with all of the members which included what to do if you find someone unconscious and how to give CPR. A variety of community projects were being undertaken including redecorating the Youth Club, repairing and redecorating doors at the Village Centre and decorating rooms at Sobell Lodge. Similarly, we have carried out small gardening jobs like building raised beds at the primary school, demolishing greenhouses, painting sheds, fences, re-felting shed roofs and occasional jungle clearance. Staplehurst became known across Kent as a highly successful model and helped many other groups looking to set up their own Shed. It was around that time that I joined.

Inevitably given the age profile, there have been health issues and some deaths among the members and their near families. Dementia has unfortunately been a particular common condition affecting several members directly and as carers. The Shed offers an opportunity to share concerns about health and personal worries, but it also gives sufferers a focus and a lift. One member with advanced Alzheimer's would regale us with stories of his career in land mine clearance before his carer took him home. Sadly, his condition deteriorated during the Covid lockdown period and, like several others, he was unable to return.

The March 2020 lockdown could have stopped everything. Nigel, recognising the importance of the weekly meetings to some members, quickly set up a Whatsap group and introduced

Zoom for weekly virtual meetings. These included involving some people who did not have a computer or smartphone by use of their normal voice telephone for Zoom. Many members were, to be kind, not very tech-savvy, but it meant that the Shed kept going and more than half of the members took part in these virtual meetings. Later, when outdoor meetings were permitted, members gathered outside the Youth Club, socially distanced. At one meeting, the conversation turned to hearing. Of the 12 men present, 11 were wearing hearing aids and unfortunately the traffic noise and the social distancing made communication very difficult. One member, Graham, a quite blunt farmer from Headcorn, got up and said, "I can't hear b**ger all!" and left. When the second Covid lockdown began in January 2021 we knew that members could at least keep in touch via the weekly Zoom and the Whatsap group was used to share some jokes and cartoons. (Before anyone wonders, these were not particularly crude or sexist.)

Nigel's unexpected death in March 2021 was shocking for us all personally. We fully recognised that Nigel was absolutely central for the Shed; he had done virtually everything; leader, treasurer, secretary, organiser of working groups, etc. Admittedly, he hadn't normally made the tea. All of the members wanted the Shed to continue and I volunteered to take over as leader on the proviso that I did not have to undertake all the other roles as well. Many other members offered to help and we were able to carry on, but unsurprisingly, without the enthusiasm and zeal that Nigel had shown.

In-person meetings were resumed for a few months from July 2021. But in December, the Youth Club was dissolved by its trustees and although the Parish Council planned to take over both the running of it and the ownership of hut, it would take some time to sort out things. Very generously, the Scouts allowed the Shed to meet in their Hut. Legalities and other things meant the Youth Club was not reopened until May 2022. By this time our pool skills, which were never very good in the first place, had deteriorated further. However, the Shed had survived. Further issues with the Youth Club building meant it was closed between October 2023 and May 2024 during which we were again very grateful to use the Scout Hut for our meetings, but we were delighted when we could return to the Youth Club.

The practical side has reduced over recent times as the age and fitness profile means that many members are no longer able or wishing to undertake much, and some have never been interested. It is to be hoped that new members will help the group undertake more things in the village, such as recently erecting a shed for the Youth Club. The Shed continues to be a place where men come together to socialise, play pool, Scrabble, share ideas and skills, participate on practical projects and make new friends. Tea and coffee are provided. Currently we have about 20 members, aged from 50 - 90, with about 15 coming each week.

The first flyer leaflet had the headline, "Join us for a cuppa." In many ways, that hasn't changed.

Speed Watch

Malcolm Buller

In 2006 Parish Councillors in the Maidstone area were invited to attend a demonstration of equipment for a new scheme recently approved for use by volunteers in Kent. Several Staplehurst Councillors went to Police Headquarters in the Sutton Road. Stood on the skid pan with their backs to an approaching car, they were asked to estimate its speed. The second run-past was unanimously thought to be faster. Turned to face the car, they still kept to their opinions. All four passes were at 30mph, the difference being the gear engaged by the driver.

The Speed Indication Device (SID) and scheme were then demonstrated, showing how the vehicle's speed could be recorded on paper, along with the registration plate, make, colour and time. Impressed, the Parish Council decided to invest around £2,000 and invite residents to take part in training sessions. Over the next few months about twenty did so and Staplehurst drivers began to realise that speeding in the village might result in a letter from the police.

I was far from impressed with the policeman's training session and, as I had taken early-retirement from teaching, I wrote to

SPEED WATCH

the Chief Constable offering to do the job. My letter was passed down the line until it ended up in Maidstone and I was invited to go into the 'Nick' for a chat with the recently appointed new leader of the scheme in this area. PC Warren Jarvis had many roles and Speed Watch was just one of them. There was no paid employment, but would I become a Police Volunteer to help Warren run the area scheme? The DBS-type checks for working inside a police station are very thorough! So is the computer training package to give access to a limited part of the County system.

Staplehurst's volunteers organised themselves into groups of three and borrowed the equipment for a couple of hours to stand in one of the designated locations. A warning triangle sign had to be placed further up the road before the team had one person facing away from the traffic to read out loud the speed displayed on the large screen. The details of speeding cars were later entered into a computer program and any repeat offenders reported to the police.

SPEED WATCH

Inside Maidstone Station I received these from the twelve participating parishes, but had to find a willing officer to access the Swansea DVLA computer. I found a weekly visit was best as I then typed up a letter to the registered owner before it was checked and signed by Warren. It was a slow process. However, by monitoring these we could see that some drivers were ignoring the letters so we could ask a local PC to be in position by the right road at the right time, resulting sometimes in points on the licence and fines from magistrates.

Another task was to aid Warren in training new volunteers and parish schemes. He focussed on the legal and safety aspects whilst I gave the practical tips from experience. We also hosted Area Meetings where each Parish Coordinator could share their thoughts and requests. We wrote newsletters and took the initiative of contacting all Police Forces in England to see if and how they had introduced Speed Watch in order to share best practice. Very few had and those involved did so in widely different ways.

SPEED WATCH

In about 2014 Kent Police was re-organised again and Speed Watch became a countywide scheme based at Road Traffic Headquarters, Coldharbour, under a senior civilian's direct control. The required policy meant great changes so I had to teach this new leader what the scheme actually involved and how the volunteers operated it. The benefits though were that any motorist recorded twice anywhere in Kent would trigger the computer system which could also check its details and issue letters. Our Maidstone practice of issuing strongly worded rebukes to any driver exceeding the limit by 50% was adopted, as well as the hand-delivery for persistent offenders by a uniformed officer. More parishes joined the scheme and our wider audience led to county conferences which I chaired.

In 2016 a new Speed Indication Device was developed which gave a vastly improved range. Grants were obtained and Staplehurst was one of the first to benefit. Speeding vehicles could now be detected at 400 metres and so volunteers had much

SPEED WATCH

more time to gather the required information. Soon afterwards, Kent joined with an improved computer scheme developed in Sussex. This made major changes to the way data was handled and new volunteers had to follow a training programme on-line and pass a test before being passed to each parish's coordinator for roadside training. The scheme was shut down during the pandemic and some meetings of coordinators are held on-line.

In 2023 the Parish received an automatic speed indication device that can be moved to different locations. The battery life means that it cannot be used on the A229 so Bathurst, Marden and Headcorn Roads have had poles fitted with brackets. This SID records every vehicle passing by times and speeds and the analysis of this informs the council's Road Safety Group. The speeds are not shown below 27 or above 40mph to deter cyclists from speeding up, or for motorists to see how fast they can record, but these are still recorded. Such information helps the Planning Committee's evidence when challenging some developers' claims.

The purpose of all of these Speed Watch activities is to remind motorists that speed limits are there for the safety of everyone. The more often volunteers can be seen, the greater will be the improvement in road safety for Staplehurst residents. Even half an hour of your time could save a life!

A Yeoman's House

Anita Thompson

Anita wrote 'The History of a Kentish Yeoman's House' as the guide book for the Brattle Farm Museum in 1990. This is a synopsis.

As Staplehurst's population grew, land was cleared on the southern slope of the limestone ridge. Lime helps heavy clay's fertility so farms and their buildings soon followed. Every building on the northern side of Plain Road (now Five Oak Lane) as part of its estate, had to pay quit-rent to Lovehurst Farm.

The square moat was a status symbol in the fourteenth century as a means of defence as well as a water and food supply and dampcourse. This farmhouse was called Brattle after the local family who were also resident in Goudhurst and Marden in the fifteenth century. In an inventory of 1570, Brattle was described as a Hall-house with an additional parlour and chamber above with two beds. There was also a buttery. Although there was no loom there were two trendles, as spinning wheels were called, and other tools for teasing wool for spinning. There were two oxen, dairy and beef cattle, horses, pigs and sheep alongside five acres of winter wheat. A decade later that house was pulled down.

Just one beam can be seen to have been used in the replacement dwelling. It must have been built by a wealthy man, probably George Jemmett in the 1580s, by the quantity of new timber used. The western side reached towards the moat and the frontage showed a jettied upper floor. The hall ceilings were solid; lined or panelled with wood or other materials with bedrooms above. At the eastern end was a timber chimney. Yeoman's houses of this vintage were known for the quality of their materials and plainness, rather than for display.

Just a few fields away opposite Saynden, was 'Le Brokis' or 'Les Brookes' where on Christmas Day 1589 Thomas Cooper was cudgelled and thrown into a ditch by Isaac Bowreman of Marden, egged on by Mary Cooper. Both were hanged for the murder.

The timber chimney at Brattle was replaced with a brick one and the hall extended to the east in about 1600, possibly to accommodate a recently married member of the family. James Jemmett had taken Mary, the daughter of the grocer, William Thunder, to the Maidstone Fair Day. They travelled on to Rochester where it cost them 15 shillings and 8 pence (78p) to get married. When they returned later that same evening, no-one believed them. They were Anabaptists so, being married away from the diocese, were reported to the Church Courts and James had to go to Canterbury with the evidence.

In 1697 Brattle was part of the Usbornes of Loddenden's empire. They had made their fortune through tanning and were the richest family in the parish. The Reeves family were tenants for many years. In 1756 William and Ann took down the western end that was so near to the moat and used the materials to build a dairy on the cooler northern side. A catslide roof facing the moat then became a kitchen with its own chimney facing west. After William's death, Ann married the miller who had built the windmill in Bell Lane.

A YEOMAN'S HOUSE

John Collinson was also a tenant, but in the 1820s when the war with France ended, bankruptcy caused by food imports hit Kent very badly. In 1830 John's creditors, his brother-in-law and William Jull (LL-SS p34) had to evict the family. John moved next door to Ashurst (LL-SS p19) as a farm labourer. In February icebergs had reached the Kent coast, hops failed and the hay crop went mouldy. Agricultural workers were so poverty-stricken that the riot act was read in Cranbrook and the Dragoons summoned from Maidstone. Farmers refused to join the Special Constables as they believed their workers should get a raise to 2 shillings and sixpence (13p) a week. By February 1831, the next tenant, Joseph Reeves, was already in debt. He carried on until finally bankrupted in 1851.

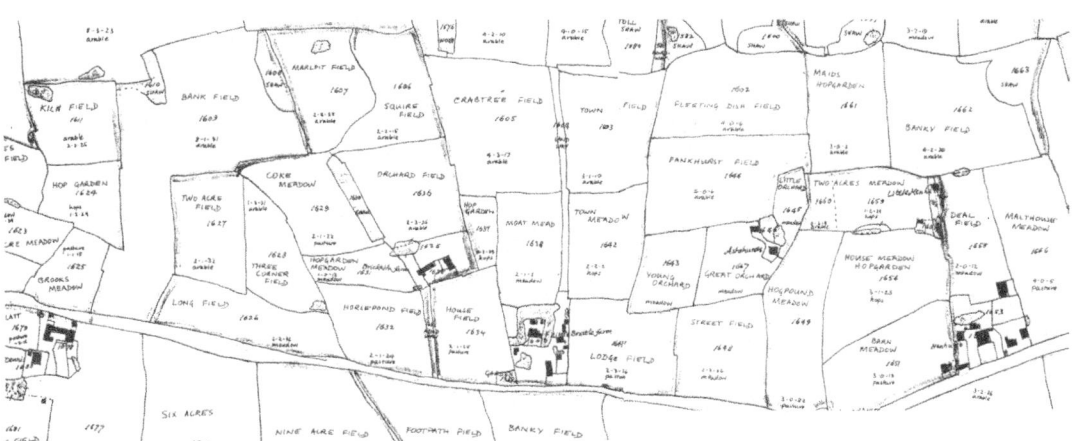

In July 1842 the official Assessment of Tithes was confirmed and a detailed map produced. This showed Brattle Farm as being of 51 acres, 3 roods and 34 perches which totalled 52.6 acres. This meant that each year the payment for tithes to the Rector of All Saints would be 9 pounds and 12 shillings (£9.60). Over two thirds of the land was under arable crops with 9 acres of grassland, 3 of the risky hops and 4 acres of woodland for fuel and timber for repairs to the house, tools or fences. By the 1851 census, Brattle had changed its name to Moat Farm and Joseph and Ann were lying about their ages.

A YEOMAN'S HOUSE

In 1861 Moat Farm housed the Usborne's Bailiff, but the adjacent farm was called Little Brattle. By the next census during the farming depression, Little Brattle Farm had reverted to Brickkiln and Moat back to Brattle, the latter being divided into two cottages housing six and seven residents. When Ann Usborne died in 1875, along with much of the Loddenden property, Brattle became part of the Hoare's Iden Park 3,000-acre estate. Due to bad investments, Henry Hoare the Younger was forced to sell in 1879. Brickkiln was demolished and the land added to Brattle Farm which was now described as an old-fashioned farmhouse with three bedrooms, a large attic, sitting room, kitchen, back kitchen, washhouse and dairy. The eastern side was an old cottage with three bedrooms, a kitchen, washhouse, pantry, dairy and woodhouse. There were many farm outbuildings, but Brattle did not sell. It was leased to the landlord of the Kings Head (formerly known as The Bell). It failed to find a buyer again in 1881, nor in 1904 even though the frontage no longer had an overhang as bricks and tiles had made it more secure; and it boasted six bedrooms.

In 1913 it finally sold to an architect, Charles Denham, who installed many modern conveniences, but he too fell bankrupt in 1929. "Old-fashioned, but recently restored at considerable expense" lured Norman Stacy to own the now four-bedroomed property with its dressing room and bathroom upstairs. There was a 34-bay cowshed and an oast house with upper cooling floors as well as other store rooms. 35 acres were now classed as pasture with another 10 of grass under apple trees. Woodland was now just 2 acres and arable crops only 11. A further 6 acres were devoted to soft fruit, destined for Covent Garden by rail. Stacy also added a telephone line and a running water supply before selling to Mr Titley in 1938. His son Reg had poor eyesight and found coping with the farm difficult.

Despite the war being fought in the skies above, Brattle survived unscathed apart for work in some northern fields in 1944 by Italian prisoners-of-war to lay the PLUTO pipeline which supplied fuel to troops in France after D-Day. One of the seven regular London commuters, Albert Thompson, bought the run-down Brattle Farm on Reg's death in 1952 and installed his 22-year-old son Brian to run it. The farmhouse had sitting tenants so the family lived in one of the recently built cottages further down the lane. Albert bought Ashurst to achieve 100 acres, but that farmhouse had been pulled down as a liability. (If only it had been there a few years later when Brian married Anita.) During the post-war years, what was farmed changed as the markets dictated. Animals came and went, as did fruit and runner beans. Cereals dominated in the 1980s, but fluctuating EEC diktats caused administrative nightmares.

Brian's passion for collecting included a whole barn from Frittenden Brickworks in 1981, but that caught fire in 1984. The water supply in the moat helped the Fire Brigade save Brattle from an even greater catastrophe. The collections grew into a fully-fledged Farm Museum centred in the oast house, with numerous

A YEOMAN'S HOUSE

out-buildings housing tractors and tools, bicycles and vintage cars, fruit and hop-growing essentials and so much more. In March 1987 Brattle Farmhouse was designated as a Grade II listed building.

The need for farmers to adjust and diversify is great. Some buildings are now let to a Florist and a Dog Grooming and Therapy business. Even the farmhouse is warmer now in 2024 (p69 poem).

Living In History

Roy Laming

I don't really know why my wife and I have always preferred living in very old properties as we both grew up in houses built in the 1930's onwards. Maybe it is the more distinctive character or the additional space that older houses often provide when compared with more recently built properties. As a soon-to-be married couple and with a need to be near a station to commute to London, our search for our first home led us down the railway line from our parents' homes in south-east London through Sevenoaks and Tonbridge until we could find something we could afford! Although our search for our first home had focused on properties nearer to the capital, the details for the pretty Victorian terraced cottage of 2 Market Street, Staplehurst landed on the doormat one day. We were immediately enchanted with the 'two-up, two-down' house, its 200-foot-long allotment style garden, the village setting and attractiveness of the surrounding area. Plus, there was the benefit of just a two-minute walk to the station and a guaranteed seat on the train for the still not-too-long journey up to London!

Market Street, on some maps as Market Place, probably takes its name from the trading site set up in about 1869 when several market traders, dissatisfied with stall prices at Ashford, set up their own market in Staplehurst. The railway provided a siding adjacent to Market Street where an engine could wait to load animals and goods. The market operated until about 1937.

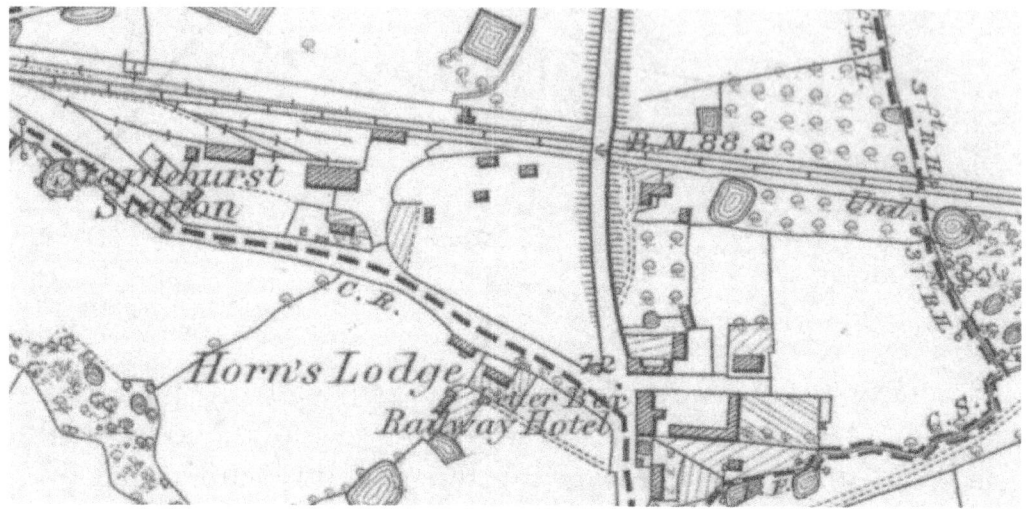

We came to learn that living in older properties would have maintenance challenges, but there is a sense of being a custodian of something built long ago and trying to preserve it as a comfortable and characterful home for future generations. We were told by our lovely neighbour Henry, a long-standing Market Street resident, that the cottages were built using sandstone blocks dug out from land near Iden Manor at the other end of the village, creating the lake that can now be found there. However, other information suggests that the mud taken to enlarge the lake at Iden Park for the banker Henry Hoare was made into concrete blocks. These were a foot thick and almost impossible to hammer a picture nail into. A sandstone building without a damp course is always going to draw in some moisture, rising up from the ground below. Thankfully, this and the other quirks of the cottage did not spoil our enjoyment of living there for our first eight years in Staplehurst.

Another characteristic of a few of the cottages in Market Street at that time was that some of their windows appear to be filled in. This was likely because a window tax, based on the number of windows in a house, was introduced in 1696 by William III. It was a banded tax according to the number of windows in the house. For example, for a house in 1747 with ten to 14 windows, the tax was 6d per window; it increased to 9d with more windows. Not long after its introduction, people bricked up their windows to avoid paying the tax! It was repealed in 1851 after pressure from doctors and others who argued that lack of light was a source of ill health. If the windows in the Market Street cottages were blocked up for this reason, then they would possibly have been built in the 1840's. The sense of community developing around Market Street at that time can also be seen from the former Market Stores that stood at the corner, which were established in 1846 as can be seen from the date plaque prominently placed at an apex of the roofline.

As our family started to expand, it became time to move on from Market Street and find a larger house. Early in our search, one of the village estate agents sent us the details of 'Victoria Cottage and Works' in Chapel Lane and so we arranged a visit. The agent warned us that the property needed much work and was somewhat wary when we turned up for a viewing with a baby in a sling. The agent was not wrong! With the amount of work needed and a price tag of £100,000 for the whole site, it was well beyond our means. However, a builder took on the task and converted and refurbished the buildings into three homes; we revisited a couple of years later and subsequently purchased the Victoria Cottage part in 1993.

The iconic photo of Victoria Cottage and Works with Mr John Harris and his workers standing outside is probably well known to many Staplehurst residents. (It heads both front covers of this series of Staplehurst Stories.) Yet there are many facets of the property which are less well known. The building actually stands on the site of one of the early schools in the village, dates back to 1832 and was probably the back part of the former wheelwright building (now 2 Wheelwrights). It was when the 'new school' (now the Community Centre) was built on the High Street in 1873 that Mr Harris moved from Frittenden and bought the property to expand his business. He extended and converted the old school to create his workshop. Then, in 1876 he built the house alongside the Works which is Victoria Cottage. When John died in 1925 his two sons Frank and Fred took over the business. A third son, Charles, had died as a result of injuries incurred in the first world war. The initials of all three sons can be found etched into the brickwork at various places at the back of the property. Remnants of the furnace and tool rack from cartwheel making days can still be seen in the part of the Works that now forms the car port to the two Wheelwrights cottages.

Newspaper snippets record events of the Harris family lives which shows they extended their community service beyond being local wheelwrights and undertakers – one time they fought a fire that had started at the rear of the former Royal Oak pub (LL-SS p202) and they also saved a woman from London who had fallen down a well! Frank Harris was an avid collector of clocks with one article recording he had 65 including a 400-day clock, a Cromwellian, a 300-year-old water clock, a skeleton clock and six grandfather clocks. All those had long since gone by the time we moved in, but it was certainly a privilege to become only the second family to live in the house and stay there for twenty-two years. However, for most of that time it was still known by many residents as the 'Harris' place'.

Having lived in the north of the village in Market Street and then right in the middle in Chapel Lane, it seems the time came for us to move south. With our three daughters having moved out and on in their lives we decided it was time to resize and one of the oldest properties in Staplehurst, Fuller Cottage on The Quarter and almost the very last house on the south-side of the village became our next home. As you can imagine, a house dating from around 1580 was bound to have more quirks and curiosities than our previous two houses, including rooms in which the floors sloped by about six inches from one side to the other.

A detailed History of Fuller House and Fuller Cottage, originally known together as just 'Fullers', would fill many pages of this book. Indeed, a lady that lived in the property in the 1990's documented its entire history, researching wills, maps and census data to create a 58-page booklet which we are fortunate to possess. The property has inevitably undergone many changes in its 440 years' history. It was likely built as a result of the wealth from the textile industry prevalent in the area at the time. It was sited and oriented to be an impressive structure with the front originally being the elevation facing towards the hill - it would be a striking sight in the distance for travellers, as they came over the hill by the Church when travelling south. From an extensive will of the owner who died in 1664, we know that by then the property had been extended to create two large gables on the eastern side which then became the front of the house facing the road.

Fullers was also subject to the 'Hearth Tax', a property tax introduced by King Charles II in 1662 to raise money to pay for the royal household. The records of 1664 show Fullers having eight hearths. Whilst not that many remain, today, a log burning fire is very welcome to combat draughts on windy days. The property was almost certainly thatched when first built to keep in the heat. One of the windows from when the house was first built is still present. It has three vertical wooden bars and, since glass had not yet been invented, would have had shutters and hessian to keep out the wind and rain. This window has been preserved in its original state as it is now on the inside of Fuller Cottage within an extension which was probably added in 1628. This date is stamped on a small window in the cat-slide roof. The historic location of other windows are indicated by the cut-outs in numerous beams and two pairs of later leaded-glass windows, taken out of the house at some point, can now be found in the garage barn.

The research into Fullers' past gives a fascinating insight to how the property has been shaped and used over time. The early evidence shows it being a fine manor house with wealthy owners with servants. Then, through the years it was often subdivided and redivided as farm workers cottages. In the grounds in the 17th century there had been a workhouse, a cheese house, a milkhouse, a brewery, a laundry and a buttery. Census records from 1851, 1861 and 1871 show the site accommodating four households, then three in 1881 and 1891, then four again in 1901 with a total of 21 people living on the site at that time. It was then three homes again before being sold as a single property in 1951, including a builder's yard and a 4.5-acre market garden. An application from December 1951 was for a change of use of one of the rooms into a café, although it seems such a facility never actually opened. Another planning application followed in 1952 to divide the property once again into two.

LIVING IN HISTORY

Today, Fullers House and Fullers Cottage are two spacious family homes which are enveloped by the charms of the original Elizabethan structure and later additions. In 2018 listed planning consent was given to build a garden room in place of an awkward small courtyard and hopefully this enhancement to Fuller Cottage will continue to be enjoyed by future generations.

Play The Game

Malcolm Buller

Many high-level footballers worked in factories during the week and played matches on Saturdays, but when World War One called them into action, women were summoned to take their places. Spectators flocked to see these games, and after the war, they continued to draw in the crowds. The Preston munitions factory produced the Dick, Kerr Ladies team who, on Boxing Day 1920, filled Everton's Goodison Park stadium with 53,000 spectators (and left another 14,000 outside) where they beat St. Helens Ladies 4-0. The match raised a huge amount for the unemployed and disabled ex-servicemen.

The owners of men's teams panicked and lobbied the Football Association who, in 1921, banned its members from being referees or linesmen at any women's games and banned females from playing on any affiliated grounds. This meant that no stadium could be used. Other countries followed this route which stayed in place in Britain until the 1970s. Despite this, some female football did happen, but very unofficially.

In 1971, Mexico could be the hosts for the women's World Cup as two large stadia were privately owned. 'The British

Independents Football Club' was formed to take part, organised by Harry Batt, a bus driver, and his wife June. They recruited from players they knew. The oldest was twenty-four and the youngest just thirteen. The Batts took the young ladies to watch a friendly match between Manchester United and Luton. The 10,000 spectators watching Charlton, Best and Law was to help their team become used to a 'big game' atmosphere. The next day they flew to Mexico where they had a police escort from the plane to their coach through the crowds and reporters, and then through the throngs lining the streets. Fans threw sweets and gifts through the open coach windows to the team.

When the girls played Argentina, over 100,000 were there to watch them lose 4-1. Leah Caleb, the thirteen-year-old striker resembled the World Cup Mascot, So-cheel, so she was called to wherever she went. The team appeared on television, were invited to cocktail parties and to stay in luxury hotels. The second match was against the hosts. One player said that the score was Mexico 4, our team 1 broken leg, 1 broken foot, 3 strained ligaments, 1 cartilage, 1 badly bruised shoulder and various other bruises, cuts, bumps and knocks. They stayed to watch the final where a fifteen-year-old scored a hat-trick in Denmark's 3-0 win before another police escort returned them to the airport.

In England, there was no reception and a couple of papers mentioned their injuries and defeats. The Women's FA banned all those players for three months and the Batts for life. However, to regain some control, the WFA organised 'England' trials and lifted the ban on the use of stadia for women's games. That enabled the first official international to be played, against Scotland. In 2019, the BBC tracked down the 14 players from 1971 and, happily healthy, reunited them.

In 1966 at Coventry Teacher Training College, Birmingham Referee's Association organised a course for students to study to become qualified referees. The trainers were shocked when four females took their seats along with about thirty young men. After discussion, they saw no valid reason to eject them. At the end of the course, the exam results showed all students had passed, except four. Can you imagine the shame of the first team's centre forward and three other men? The national press insisted on the girls wearing their PE kit for the photographs, but there was no route for them to pursue a career in refereeing, much to the relief of the one who lives in Staplehurst!

Factual source 'Everything to Play For – The QI Book of Sports' by J Harkin & A Ptaszynski published by Faber & Faber 2023

If Only I Could

Laura Baker-Fawcus

When I began playing football, it was as a kick-about in the garden with my older brothers. They used to take the ball past me with ease and it frustrated me. I wanted to be as good as them and better!

As I grew up and started at primary school, I realised that it wasn't the norm for a girl to play. I was always playing with the boys and that was okay with me. Sadly, not everyone understood that. Comments were made by some of my peers, all of the way through my youth. Am I a boy because only boys play football?...... I was determined not to let it phase me. I loved football and I usually wasn't afraid to show it. I would play at every given opportunity; in the garden; at the Jubilee Field (usually with my brothers' friends or the boys in my year, using coats for the goal posts); in the school playground; anywhere! I spent hours performing 'keepy-ups', dribbling, shooting etc. I knew it wasn't likely to get me anywhere, but it was fun. I can't pretend that I didn't spend much of my time imagining. If I scored in any game, I had scored the winning goal on the last day of the first division (obviously now the premiership) or the FA cup!

I persevered at primary school and finally made it into the B team of Staplehurst Primary School, along with another girl who wanted to be goalie. I found that I never quite played as well as when just playing with my friends, just in break times and lunch times. There was no pressure then so it allowed me to play freely and not worry about having to prove myself. I think my confidence was lacking at times due to being the only girl on the pitch. It sometimes seemed like such an uphill struggle. I still remember one of my biggest regrets was shooting from just outside the box in a match and it hit the crossbar! So close!

As I progressed into secondary school, I was disappointed to find the same struggle in P.E and extra-curricular sport. "Girls don't play football." Don't get me wrong, I loved any sport and so I made sure I was also in the rounders team and basketball team, but I used to complain bitterly that we couldn't play football. There was a teacher who had herself played for Exeter University ladies' team. I used to ask constantly if it was possible to play. The problem she had was trying to get another girls' team for us to play against! By Year 8 she realised I was serious so she really tried and said we could get a team together! She managed to secure a game against Maplesden Noakes where we thrashed their team 9-2. I scored a tap in, but it was one of the best moments of my footballing life; still to this day! I was lucky that a caretaker, who also had a son in my year, was prepared to take a class after school and my friends made sure I could go too. This was another way to show I was serious and not too bad a player. We managed to find a couple more schools to play against and we became a regular team.

In the meantime, I was also given the opportunity to play for a Maidstone side that was in an up-and-coming league of girls. The sport was growing, at last! There was also an opportunity to play for Club Brazil when I was in my mid-teens. It was a woman's team in its infancy that trained at the Jubilee. The difficulty was ensuring that enough women would come every week. It folded, sadly, but the games we played were fun and there was some real talent there.

I trained with Charlton and a few other teams, but I think in my heart, knowing I was never going to be able to make a career out of it meant that my determination, as I got older, waned. I put my hands up and say it was from part laziness and part love of going out partying and not making all of the sacrifices it takes to be a real player! However, I used to tell everyone who would listen, (I knew it would be at a time when I was past playing and therefore unable to make it professionally) that ladies' football would be big and we would get the recognition the sport deserves; not just in the big leagues, but at grass roots too where it belongs. My only sadness is that I never got to play for the mighty Staplehurst Monarchs, but I am so proud that we have amazing, even groundbreaking ladies' and girls' teams now!

Up the Monarchs!

Kick Off

Jess Burchell

In May 2016 following a year of training with my primary school team, at the age of 9, I decided that it was time for me to act on my love of football and join a grassroots team. However, I encountered a slight problem: there were no girls' teams in my local area. This confused me as my village's team (Staplehurst Monarchs) was huge! How could they not have a girls' section? I decided that I wanted to do something about this so I wrote a letter to the Monarchs' Club Secretary asking if they could start a girls' team for me to join. Fortunately, Staplehurst Monarchs were incredibly supportive and said that if I could find players then they would set up a team for us. Overjoyed by the news, I told my mum who helpfully put up a post on Facebook advertising for any players and within an hour we had many enquiries from young girls of all skill levels who wanted to join a team.

On the 26th May 2016, the first training session of the current Monarchs' girls' section took place. Nine girls between the ages of 7 and 9 attended and whilst this may not seem like many, as someone who was not even able to access a team a few months before, this was a massive step towards what the girls' section looks like now. With only nine players, obviously we were not able to join a league or play competitively, but we were all committed to training together so that's what we did. For one year we trained regularly, improving our skills, our team spirit and gathering new players for our team. Once we had enough, we started to play friendlies against other local sides and whilst we didn't win much, we played every game with smiles on our faces and that's all that matters. In preparation for our first season in a league, we competed in the Paddock Wood Tournament in 2017. This opportunity opened our eyes to the quality of other girls in our local area and it was an amazing opportunity to finally compete against other teams, though we were not successful.

Our first season competing in the Kent Girls' and Ladies' Football League started in September 2017, and it was everything I could have ever dreamt of. We had committed players, two willing managers and incredibly supportive parents - we were just missing the wins! Whilst we waited for the victories to start rolling in, we continued to train and play matches with smiles on our faces, week in week out for four years. In the meantime, more girls' teams were set up by Staplehurst Monarchs and we gradually grew to have five different age groups before the Covid Pandemic hit in 2020. We obviously could not train as a team for many months, but each player was committed to working individually at home so when we finally joined up as a team we had each improved massively. This became very obvious when the league restarted in 2021. In 2021/22 we had our best ever season. We came second in the league and only had three losses across the whole season. However, this also marked our last season as a team - talk about finishing on a high! This was a bittersweet moment as so many of us had stuck with the team since the beginning, but we were all moving on with our lives following the completion of our GCSEs in the summer of 2022.

Even though I do not play for Staplehurst Monarchs FC anymore, I will forever be grateful for their support throughout my journey to become a qualified referee back in 2020 which has since enabled me to officiate games in the FA Women's National League - something I couldn't even dream of! Even with my recognition from the FA and being part of the FA Women's Refereeing Emerging Talent Programme, it is always a pleasure when I am able to go back to my roots and referee matches for the Monarchs. It is absolutely amazing to see first-hand the opportunities that they offer for young girls who want to play football - with seven girls' teams and one women's team, it is reassuring to know that young girls have access to play football and won't have to face the same challenges that I did back in 2016.

Train Crash

Malcolm Buller

The idea for a steam engine was first recorded a few years BC and worked on in various forms through the centuries that followed. In 1712, Thomas Newcomen's Atmospheric Engine successfully used steam to pump water out of coal mines and this fuelled the minds of other inventors. Richard Trevithick came up with the first working locomotive when, in 1804, it hauled a train along a tramway in Wales. George and Robert Stephenson are credited with the first passenger service on the Stockton to Darlington line in 1825. Their company made most of the engines as networks spread throughout Britain, Europe and the USA.

The route from the capital to the ports linking England to the continent was refused passage through Kent's County Town so the line instead came to Staplehurst. The station was opened on 31st August 1842 when the almost straight section from Tonbridge to Headcorn was completed. The enormous volume of mail engendered by the introduction of the universal penny postage rate in 1840 needed Staplehurst, with its north to south road, to serve as the distribution centre for the whole area from Gravesend to Hastings. By 1875 sidings provided goods yards and a coal depot. The station platforms were spaced to ensure that passengers who were crossing the tracks did so behind the trains. (The first footbridge was not installed until 1969.)

Many Victorians who could afford to do so would use the train to escape from London's crowded streets and travel via Folkestone to the space afforded by France. Such travellers returning by ship were at the mercy of the tides, but such was the importance of this route, the extra 'Boat' or 'Tidal Train', provided by the South Eastern Railway, would be waiting for them. The journey from Paris to London was so much quicker than the horse-drawn vehicles of yesteryear, even if the engines travelling at 50 miles per hour were smelly and smoky. Passengers leaving Paris at 7am would be across the channel and boarding their 'special' by 2:30pm, ready for their journey through the Garden of England.

The straight line of the track gave excellent vision for Crombie, the driver, as he guided the powerful engine westwards through Headcorn. John Wiles was standing beside the track, as he had done so for the last three months, ten telegraph poles to the east of the river bridge. None of the team working on the line had realised that these poles were much closer together than normal. He saw the steam some three miles away and started waving his red flag and shouting. He realised that this was the tidal train approaching; two hours ahead of schedule. The foreman, Henry Benge, and his team had been working on the bridge that carried the rails across the River Beult on sturdy wooden beams which they were replacing one-by-one. The long rails were removed, the beam changed and the rails replaced before the next train was due. But on this Friday, 9th June 1865, Henry read the time for the tidal train from the Saturday line. Henry was 33, earnt a guinea a week (3 shillings for the extra responsibility) but could not read or write very well and had never been issued with a company watch as he should have been.

The train was about a mile away when the workers were alerted to it and ran and jumped for their lives. The driver gave two blasts on his whistle, shut off the steam and applied the brakes. The momentum of the engine, the tender, fourteen carriages, a luggage van and the brake car had only diminished by about 20mph when the train reached the bridge. Workers could only watch as the engine flew the twenty-one feet and return to the rails. It dragged the tender, brake van and two first-class carriages with it. A cast-iron girder snapped under the impact and a carriage hung over the gaping hole into which the next eight carriages plunged. Another was teetering on the precipice, held by the remainder of the train, stationary behind.

The summer river was not deep, but the Wealden clay bed was like glue. Passengers started to emerge from the wreckage of the shattered carriages and residents from Headcorn, Hawkenbury and Staplehurst were quickly travelling to their aid. Climbing from one of the teetering carriages with a half bottle of brandy was a celebrity figure. Charles Dickens had been abroad with his mistress, Ellen Ternan, and her mother, but now he was trying to comfort the wounded. He was reported to have used his top hat to scoop water from the river to bathe wounds or give drinks, neither of which sounds sensible. He returned to the train and helped the ladies to escape and clamber down to the river bank, before returning to collect his manuscript for 'Our Mutual Friend'. Twenty medical men got to the scene and one, Mr Wilkins, a Staplehurst surgeon, turned his house into a hospital. Others offered accommodation to the injured. Frederick Watson, a hairdresser living in Crown Cottages, was soon there with his camera to take the three shots from the same spot. In all, there were ten fatalities and fifty injured amongst about a hundred and ten passengers.

A hundred and fifty men were needed to make the necessary repairs to re-open the line during Sunday morning. Meanwhile, at 4pm on the Saturday in the Railway Hotel, Staplehurst, an inquest was held. Company rules were stated to be that five sets of detonators had to be placed at two-hundred-and-fifty-yard intervals when rails were removed with the flagman therefore a thousand yards from the work. Joseph Gallimore, the district inspector said he had never asked Benge if detonators were being used. The coroner charged them both with manslaughter and exonerated Wiles and Crombie. When appearing later at the Cranbrook Magistrates' Court, Gallimore's solicitor said that as his client had twenty gangs to oversee, he couldn't be everywhere at once and that if rules weren't followed, that would be the fault of senior men. Benge's solicitor failed to turn up so he could only say sorry for his mistake. They were both committed for trial on bail. At a Board of Trade enquiry in July, Gallimore was found to have either known the rules were not being followed, but if not, then he was at fault for not knowing. Both pleaded not guilty at the Kent Summer Assizes. Giving evidence, the Head Engineer said that, against the rules, the company had never given out watches to foremen. After a short retirement, the judge instructed the jury to find Gallimore acquitted. However, Benge was found guilty and sentenced to nine months hard-labour.

Charles Dickens was badly affected by the crash. He lost his voice for two weeks, hated train travel and at his home at Gad's Hill, Kent, on the fifth anniversary, June the 9th 1870, he died.

Day To Day In Australia

Val Hoddinott

Dave and I lived in Australia for nearly seven years and, like all visitors, we were keen to look at everything around the mighty continent. We explored for thousands of miles by road and track – the west, north and east coasts, the red centre, and from South Australia journeyed west across the barren Nullabor Plain to Perth and the Indian Ocean. All was so vast – and empty – and hot – and awesome! My memories now include riding a camel along the 80-mile beach in Broome, Western Australia and boat rides to see whales, dolphins and a pearl farm. In the Northern Territory we visited Kimberley and took a helicopter trip over the Bungle Bungles and a diamond mine; Kakadu and swimming in a rock pool at night in Mataranka; toasting marshmallows around a camp fire at Uluru (Ayers Rock) and the two of us walking alone around the entire base of the monolith. Moving on we panned for gem stones at Emerald in Queensland, stopping for a break in South Australia and peering down over the heights of the Australian Point at a huge whale swimming with her baby immediately beneath me in the Great Southern Ocean. How wonderful was that?

But life needs us to keep our feet on the ground and happens day to day – without all of that adventure!

On arrival in Western Australia I felt I wanted to live in an older house – maybe with its own gum tree. We visited another fishing town, Mandurah, 50 kilometres south of Perth. The fishing industry had ended some years before, but Mandurah crabs are renowned throughout Western Australia so a 'Crab Festival' is held annually. There was lots of fun, noise and excitement, not least during the Chinese Dragon Boat racing in the harbour. It was quiet when we arrived and sat by the harbourside for breakfast. There were dolphins swimming – not six feet away from us! That was it! I'd found where I wanted to live.

The house we chose had several gum trees and also poinsettias, jacaranda, wattle and palm trees in just under an acre of 'old Australia'. I hadn't anticipated the birds and animals – they all came as a wonderful and unexpected surprise.

DAY TO DAY IN AUSTRALIA

It was January, mid-summer, so we sat outside in the garden having breakfast and tossing crumbs to the birds (an English custom frowned on by many Australians). These two or three Australian Magpies had soon invited their friends to join us so we were feeding about two dozen. They expected to be fed at sunrise each morning and gathered at the kitchen door. No alarm clocks were needed as windows were open to the air – and noise! To my joy, we found that Kookaburras also relished a feed of minced beef and would take it from your hand. Three came to call each springtime and it was daunting at first to offer a hand to such a large beak, but there were never any injuries. Dave planted potatoes at the end of the garden and when digging he was accompanied by a Fairy Wren. It was small with a long tail, bright blue and dazzling in the sunshine, with quick, darting movements through the bushes. Dave walked side-by-side in the garden with his own special friend.

Every evening at dusk we had the squawking frog chorus which we relayed by phone to our family in the UK. They croaked endlessly, but were rarely seen. One little one strayed into the deep end when our pool was being constructed. When rescued and placed back on to the garden soil, he promptly started digging backwards, disappearing bottom-first. There was also a very ugly, solid lizard about eight inches long and with a huge mouth, called a Blue Tongue, for obvious reasons. One afternoon I almost stepped on it as I walked through the front door. In terror, the poor creature dashed into the house. It could have gone anywhere! I was terrified. Where was Dave? Of course he was playing at the local Bowls Club. I rang my neighbours for help! My hero came round with a tea towel, caught the lizard and wrapped it up to carry it safely outside. I went off to the shops and bought cat food to make amends to the lizard, but fed it regularly, not on the doorstep, but at the far end of the garden.

Most Australians are wary of the proximity of possums to their homes because they have the reputation for invading roof spaces. Ours though slept in a bush alongside our bedroom window and always enjoyed the offer of a small bunch of grapes. It was no trouble at all. At the local tearooms customers were daily entertained by their resident possum being offered a slice of bread and jam. It always climbed down from its tree to accept and eat it, much to everyone's delight.

From time to time, we had three or four larger birds with long, curved bills, visiting our garden. These Common Ibis moved slowly and silently. I'd heard of the Sacred Ibis of Egypt, but mine were every bit as special. In the U.K. we're used to seeing ducks swimming in the water and grazing on the grass or scoffing down bread. I was not prepared for the mother duck who walked through our garden at 4pm and promptly flew up to settle in the branches of our gum tree. Her following tribe of little ducklings very soon followed her upwards to sit happily above many predators. They were a sight to see! Trees are home to many creatures and if you prise away the dead leaves of palm trees you will invariably disturb three or four chunky, blue lizards who will scamper away before you can catch them.

I have so many memories of each day at home in Australia. I was so fond of the pelicans at the waterside; so sorry to leave Australia with those lovely days and star-dusted skies at night; truly a paradise on earth!

Journeys

Alan & Elsie Baum, Doreen Braganza, Joan & Malcolm Buller, Dorothy Crooks, Alan Gregory, Bob Ham, Mary Moran, Chris Ralph, Pat Sherlock & Jennie Sweetman

A recorded Interest Group morning raised many laughs as we marvelled at the journeys and their consequences. As always, one tale reminded others of their own experience. Some other stories could not be included because of 'noises off' or because it came from a non-resident of Staplehurst.

When 'package holidays' were new in the early 70s, we were excited to book to go abroad. We drove to the Leeds airfield, into an open car park and walked the twenty yards to the terminal building. Our car would stay there for the fortnight, for free. The building was an old aircraft hangar with a stone floor and basic facilities. We checked in, weighed our luggage on one of those machines with the large red dial showing the weight and within half an hour we had boarded our aircraft. It was an old Dakota; all metal, without a smidgen of padding or upholstery and no luxuries. The in-flight refreshments amounted to a boiled sweet on take-off. We landed in Southend; to re-fuel. When we reached Switzerland, we were given an envelope which contained two rail tickets, but no instructions. It was an area of the country where German, French and a mixture language were spoken, so our school-day French was of little help. The change of trains got us to Montreux, but then we found that we had to board a mountain railway in order to reach the hotel. When we arrived at our stop, it was just a shed, but there, about thirty yards away, was our hotel. However, to get to it we had to cross a plank-and-rope bridge. The hotel was really beautiful (it having been a TB Hospital all of the beds were hospital beds) but every room had a large balcony with wonderful views.

My father loved boats and hired a cruiser on the Norfolk Broads. It was when you could moor virtually anywhere and life was tranquil. It was so cold that we had to wear every item of clothing we had with us. However, as an enthusiastic teenager, I was being helpful, emptying the teapot over the side, having forgotten to take the lid off first.

A red double-decker bus was departing so I ran to catch it. "Jump!" called out the conductor. I did and grabbed the rail safely. Then I discovered that it was the wrong bus.

JOURNEYS

I had been persuaded against my better judgement to help a 'friend' by teaching young students who were on day-release from their courses. One session was maths and the other was computing. I was provided with a Sinclair ZX Spectrum as I had zero knowledge (or interest) in computing. Having left school to go into hairdressing and the like, the last thing these teenagers wanted were classroom lessons. Some refused to take part and others played games. One already had GCSE computing. They had to turn up to get their ticks, but they all hated it, nearly as much as I did. I resigned, but had to work out my notice. It was at the end of a tedious day when I got on the bus in the dark in Maidstone and it was sometime before I realised that the journey seemed different. I asked the driver where we were and he explained patiently that this wasn't the number 5, but a shuttle around the small villages and that I owed money for the extra mileage I was travelling. (I didn't have any as I kept cash to a minimum with the students I had.) When we reached the end stop, I had to ask if he could let me have 10p to phone home. He was kind and had seen how distressed I was. About an hour late, my message was, "Don't ask. Come and get me. Entrance to Marden Station!"

JOURNEYS

In 1973 my husband worked for Castrol, organising exhibitions, and was away for long periods and, as that was the time our first child was born, the company decided we deserved a holiday in Kenya, but without our daughter. At Heathrow we were shown to lovely seats on a Jumbo Jet to fly to Nairobi. We were met on arrival and told that our connection to Mombasa had been missed so we and all of our luggage should get in the jeep to be taken to another part of the airfield. After miles we arrived beside the tiniest plane I had ever seen. The pilot said that we had to wait a bit because a chap was coming with a can of fuel. A wad of paper money was given and we got into the two seats behind the pilot, expecting to take off. We had to wait for something else. There were no more seats, but soon another chap arrived with six crates of live chickens. Our flight was slow, despite the wing power of the chickens, and we seemed to dust the tops of all the trees on the way. We were met in Mombasa and driven to our opulent hotel. We had a hire car and were able to see the wonderful country, but I would never wish to go there again. The

contrast between the hotel life and that of the Kenyans was stark, exemplified by the hotel staff who were smart and attentive, but lived in mud huts outside the barbed-wire hotel perimeter.

Two days after I returned from Mombasa, I had to see Dr Gildeh because I had horrendous stomach problems. A sample was sent in for analysis and I was taken into Maidstone Hospital's Intensive Care Unit. After some days a consultant said that it was still unclear what the problem was, but they thought a bug had attached itself to my intestine. That got dealt with and after some days I was told that it was miraculous that I hadn't lost my kidneys and caused other damage, so I could go home. And that's why I won't go back there either!

A two-week school trip to the Masai Mara for 12 to 14-year-olds was an experience. We stayed in a tented village and had to spend one day with a tribe. We were greeted with lovely singing and dancing, instructions as to where we could stand safely and how to milk a cow. Then the boys went off with the men whilst the girls stayed to work with the women. They expected to be making beautiful beaded crafts so were more than dismayed when their job was to help make a hut for a new bride with their bare hands out of cow dung. Later tasks were not quite as daunting to them. When the boys got back from standing on one leg, holding a pole whilst watching the cattle, they were delighted to have been shown how to make bows and arrows and throw spears. Back at our camp, these were being demonstrated and, being the first aider, I was called upon to practise needlework on a child's arm.

A demonstration of jumping fascinated visitors. The Masai warriors made their shoes from old tyres and one boasted he could jump so high because his were Pirellies. Several other members recalled wonderful experiences of the country, the wonderful wildlife, the happy, smiling people and luxury tents; a country they'd return to any day.

JOURNEYS

Father was in the RAF and we moved regularly from base to base so I have always loved to watch the planes overhead. The sound of one type has thrilled me the most. As I grew up, I learnt to fly gliders and some small light aircraft, but never stayed anywhere long enough to gain enough hours for a pilot's licence. My family have known about this and so for my eightieth birthday present, they took me to Headcorn Aerodrome for a flight in a Spitfire. You have to wear the big, heavy boots and flying gear, have a parachute on your back and be given training ready for any escape and safe landing without the plane. Meeting Parky, one of the Battle of Britain flight pilots, was special and I was excited to sit in with him. The roar of that engine is something else!

Having flown over Staplehurst, we headed for Dover, in and out of cloud, seeing the countryside spread out below, and then the English Channel. Parky said it was time to head back so we came over the Dover Harbour and White Cliffs and then asked if I'd like to take the controls. It wasn't a hard decision. I now realise how those young men during the war could learn to fly so quickly. The control stick is just in front of you and a quarter of an inch movement takes you up, down or to the sides. Coming back to Ashford Parky asked if I wanted to do a roll. What about a loop-the-loop? "Yeeesss!" It was wonderful. As we came back to the airfield where my family were all gathered to see us land, he asked, "Shall we do it again?" They couldn't believe the loop-the-loop and roll before we landed before their eyes. It was the most wonderful flight ever. Do I next have a wing-walk or parachute jump?

Having nearly drowned as a child, I have always feared travelling on water. When Dad took the family on a boat trip round the bay, I stayed on the beach to 'guard the bags'. Years later however, as my brother was a teacher on an RAF base in Germany near the Dutch border, our sons travelled out to him as soon as Cranbrook School closed for the summer and we followed when we had finished work. I was so scared to board the Olau Line's ferry at Sheerness for the seven-hour voyage. Having calmed down, I began to appreciate the luxury of what seemed a five-star hotel and even enjoyed taking in the sights from being out on deck. Having the car enabled many journeys, but one was an evening trip to see the nightjars, a bird I had never seen before. The eight of us parked off the road on a track in woodland and followed my brother to an open field where we stood. As dusk fell, we all waved our white handkerchiefs as he assured us the birds would think they are their favourite large moths. In the pitch dark, as we returned disillusioned towards our cars, we were shouted at by two large Germans in lederhosen and brandishing rifles. Our exit was rather rapid.

Travelling overnight on the Olau line in December to attend a ship launching, we had a cabin and woke the next morning to strange noises; scraping and crunching. We emerged on to a snow-and-ice-covered deck to find the sea too had an icy surface.

For a significant birthday, I booked a hot-air-ballon flight, but because it is so weather dependent, it was nine months before the call came in to say we could go. When we arrived at Headcorn Aerodrome we met a family of four, and the pilot who said he was a member of the House of Lords. The seven of us helped prepare the balloon and basket and when we took off, we flew over Benenden Church, using the pull chord to give a burst of flame to lift us up. There was champagne to drink and it was serene floating in silence over the countryside. The pilot had a mobile phone and had to ask for the permission of landowners ahead to land. Eventually receiving a yes, he contacted Headcorn to send the vehicle to collect everything. We landed successfully

and then had to help deflate the balloon and pack everything before the trip back. The whole experience was wonderful.

Paragliding has also been a great experience. In Thailand I had the chance to float above many of the scenes from the James Bond movies. Photographs were taken of us and when I returned two years later, I was recognised and got to sail up into the warm air again. Manston was also a place to have flights, in many different craft, gliders, light aircraft and chinook helicopters.

I went riding an elephant on Christmas Day, down to the river where I bathed him.

When the East Midlands Airport was opening near Castle Donnington, my friend and I got jobs there. After the Duke of Edinburgh had done his part, we were told we had earned a free flight to Paris on Skyways. When the day came, we got aboard and were told that as the weather was bad, we couldn't land at Beauvais where the coach was, so we would go to Lydd in Kent instead. "Where's Kent?" A little plane eventually took us on, but when we arrived at the hotel, they'd relet the rooms.

JOURNEYS

The date came for my driving test exam whilst I was in college. As I hadn't ridden my Lambretta for months, I hitch-hiked home for the weekend, played in a football match and set off on Sunday after lunch. The November air was chilly and I had a frosty welcome in the elegant tearoom when I ordered a pot for one in my layers of leather. The hundred plus miles took me many hours, but I did catch the tail of chef's soggy chips. Returning home at the end of term meant the back seat and carrier were loaded with a large, heavy suitcase. The next day was thankfully warmer as I explained to the examiner that the kickstart didn't work so I had to run along beside the machine, bump start it and jump on. I managed to stall when turning right at the crossroads, but impressed him with my emergency stop when he stepped out from behind a tree. I passed.

Two pairs of us walked in relay from Paddock Wood to London in aid of Children in Need. On the last leg, in the dark as we neared the finish, we came to a bus queue beside the Old Kent Road and when we asked for donations, all but one of them turned away. The lady in an old, scruffy coat got her purse out and tipped it upside down into our bucket. "I can walk," she said and marched off.

Ron's Visit

Malcolm Buller

Ron and Dorothy Hegarty arrived in Staplehurst in 1963 and in 1971, tired of commuting, he joined the Kent Messenger Group in Week Street, Maidstone and then in their new premises in Larkfield. After he moved on to other employments, he became their part-time, Staplehurst Newshound, a position he held for a record 38 years until he retired at 75. He joined the Parish Council for twelve years in 1979 where Joan got to know him. They were both involved in setting up the early computer website for the Council with Linton Schwarz. Ron was an integral part of so many village activities and organisations, and always had an eye open for a good story!

As 'Village Correspondent', Ron contributed details of events coming up each week in the 'Village News' columns, even managing to do so from a hospital bed or whilst holidaying in Australia. He was grateful to receive our Interest Group programme so could always include weekly items. One that caught his eye was a visit to Marden Bowls Club to try out the game. Ron asked if he and Dorothy could join us. Soon after we arrived at the green, the rain started. We had a lovely welcoming chat from Martin, the Club Captain, followed by a detailed 'filler' from

RON'S VISIT

Geoff, the Groundsman, who explained all of the processes behind preparing and keeping the surface fit for play. With by now, no chance of play, we were grateful for the tea and cakes provided and several of us returned a short while after for a Saturday Open-Day experience of playing. Subsequently, at least five of us became members, including Ron, Dorothy and myself, playing during the summer and inside the pavilion during the cooler months.

In 2004 Ron came along to our group, which had just started meeting in the United Reformed Church (LL-SS p87) Schoolroom, and gave us a talk about the production of the Kent Messenger. He suggested that the group might like to go on a visit to their premises in Larkfield which he could arrange. It would have to be in an evening after most staff had left. It was early autumn and there was some rain as we parked our cars. Ron talked as he led us through the building, introducing some staff who added snippets.

RON'S VISIT

Large computer monitors were attached to keyboards and their boxes with many cables around the desks and we could imagine the noise when telephone conversations would all be going on throughout the room.

However, the noise we were hearing was coming from the roof. A sudden cloudburst had hit and the rain drops sounded as if they were demanding admittance. They were and they succeeded. Frantic action broke out as metal wastepaper buckets were tipped out and placed under torrents, aimed at drowning the computers. It was bedlam and we could only stand aside and watch.

Ron moved us down to the print room where we were amazed at the size of the rolls of paper and the machinery to handle these. The speed of printing, cutting and folding to bring each individual newspaper into existence was fantastic. Our last place to go to was the canteen where a helping of delicious chips was very welcome. A memorable visit came to an end by wading through the floods to reach the cars and trust that the roads back to Staplehurst would be passable.

One that is passable is the spine road of the recently built site off of the roundabout in the Marden Road. It was named Hegarty Way to commemorate the many contributions Ron, ably assisted by Dorothy, had made to Staplehurst.

Joiners and Ceilers

Jean Smith

The Romans established a trading port in Londinium in about 47 AD, but that was attacked and sacked by Boudica's forces around 60 AD. However, by the end of that century, Londinium was the largest settlement and soon replaced Colchester as the capital of Roman Britannia. By the time the London Wall was built, plague, fire, decay and neglect had led to an almost deserted city. It was King Alfred the Great who restored the walled city with a street plan and quays along the river front. The City of London was one of the few places where the English retained some authority when William the Conqueror granted a charter in 1075. This status entitles the City to elect a Lord Mayor, chosen by liverymen.

There are 111 livery companies in London alone, the earliest of which date probably from before the Norman Conquest. Guilds (or mysteries, from the Latin 'misterium', meaning professional skill) flourished throughout Europe for many centuries. The word 'guild' derives from the Saxon word for payment, since membership of these fraternities was (and still has to be) paid for. The word 'livery' refers to uniform clothing as a means of identification. The early livery companies were the medieval equivalent of trading standards departments, checking the quality of goods and weights and measures. They also controlled imports, set wages and working conditions as well as training apprentices. As members aged, they too were looked after and many guilds erected alms-houses. After many years of fierce dispute, an order of precedence for livery companies was finally settled, apart from the Skinners and the Merchant Taylors who were always arguing as to who were more important. In 1484 Alderman Billesden ordered that each year they alternate; and they've been "at sixes and sevens" ever since! One Mercer who died in 1423 left property worth £6,000 for alms-houses, but Richard Whittington is more often better known for his cat.

The Armorial Bearings

Fusters were carpenters in Roman times, then known as carvers and then joiners. Caelatores were the carvers in Rome, and then known as ceilers. "Joiners and Ceilers" were similar crafts, often working with saddlers who stretched leather over wooden saddle bows. The Joiners and Ceilers Guild is ranked at 41. The

Guild consists of Apprentices, Liverymen and Freemen (of the City of London). Freemen are entitled to come and go through the City gates, drive their flock across London Bridge and be hung by a silk cord instead of a rope. The Guild is organised by a Court of Assistants, Clerk, Renter Warden, Upper Warden and the Master.

When I was fifteen, I used to catch a bus with a friend along the country lanes to go to the hotel in East Tilbury on a Monday where they held a dance. I was keen on the latest craze, Rock-and-Roll, and there I met a young soldier, home on leave from his

JOINERS AND CEILERS

National Service. He was into the ballroom styles, but was keen to get to know me, so said he would go to fetch his Dad's car to drive me home. I had no intention of doing so, so my friend and I left to catch the early bus because I was under strict orders to be home by ten o'clock. Brian was persistent, and we were very surprised when we found out that our Mums already knew each other. We married in 1960 and after renting for a couple of years, bought a house in Rainham. Someone introduced Brian to the Livery Company and he was appointed its Clerk in 1964. Livery banquets were important social events for the young liverymen (and their wives) as it was an opportunity to meet interesting people like the actor Alan Bates.

JOINERS AND CEILERS

At one event the Chaplain introduced Brian to a priest and a rabbi, but I was sent into panic when I heard they had all been invited to dinner. What did each of those people eat? Going on a Cordon-Bleu course was very helpful, afterwards. As son Nigel grew up, he was introduced to livery ways by offering drinks or cigars at such times. Catering at home for the increasing numbers of guests was becoming difficult so we moved to a larger property in Bostall Heath.

Brian was a quantity surveyor in Westminster and he bought a building in Woolwich for an office and yard. He decided to specialise in gold leaf and this brought him work in prestigious hotels. As his reputation grew, he worked at both the Houses of Parliament and Buckingham Palace, where, having the right badge affixed to the front of your car, ensured you could drive straight in. Brian was also elected to the Institute of Directors and this brought him work from other sources, but not all of it was straightforward. John Paul Getty III wanted his bedroom overlooking Hyde Park decorated with brown paper which is almost impossible to stick to walls without the adhesive soaking through.

For each guild, social and craft life revolved around a parish church. St. James, Garlickhythe, was mentioned in a 12th century will and by 1375 there was certainly a guild, made up of freemen of the Joiners company there. (Hythe means a landing place and garlic was sold here.) Henry VIII introduced the recording of births, marriages and deaths and the oldest surviving registers are those of St. James, the first entry being the baptism of Edward Butler on November 18th 1535. Queen Elizabeth I granted a charter to the guild which is housed in the Guildhall. In 1578 they purchased the bible which has 'breeches' written where 'apron' usually is in Genesis 3 verse 7. It is a treasured artefact.

St James was one of many buildings destroyed by fire in 1666. It was rebuilt by 1683, but lacked a steeple. It was 33 years later that the steeple was started, but the church body boasts, at forty feet, the highest of any of Christopher Wren's interiors. During the blitz of London, a 500lb bomb crashed through the roof, mirrored in 1991 when a crane also demolished much of the building. Our Christmas card was the artist's view of the devastation, hoping for some donors to help fund repairs and allow services to resume. However, the chaplain was always keen to keep order and chatty wives were reprimanded, or even sent to the choir stalls. From here, the procession would wend its way to the livery hall behind the bible with everyone firmly in their allotted place. Nosegays were carried (to ward off the plague) and this always bemused tourists who often shouted, "What you doin'?"

Brian was very young to be elected Master in 1991 and I was too to take on the many roles. We received our medals of office and it was daunting, having to make an acceptance speech in the Mansion House. Another task included controlling the 'catty' wives. When one 'lady' was not satisfied with the bouquet allotted to her, she threw it across the room. Brian calmly walked across, picked it up and said, "Excuse me Madam. You appear to have

dropped this." Raising three children and home cooking for business clients, polishing all the livery silver in the vaults beneath the Guildhall or 'invisible mending' the ceremonial robes were very time consuming, but there were also many banquets to organise in the Mansion House and attend at other Guilds. The St George's Day Banquet in the Guildhall really went with a bang. It was at the time of the IRA action and the nearby explosion caused the chandeliers to shake, yet all 573 guests continued to enjoy their meal with a stiff upper-lip. At the banquet of the Guild of Air Pilots and Air Navigators in November 1991 I was detailed to look after a lady called Helen Sharman. I was much more nervous of this task than of many others. Yes, she was the same Helen Sharman who in May that year had become the first British person in space when she flew with two Russian cosmonauts to the Mia Space Station. Back on Earth, in the summer Helen had been asked to officially open the Summer Universiade in her home town of Sheffield. Live on international television, as she ran across the infield, she tripped over a cable and smashed the torch. Gathering the embers, she kept her cool and lit the flame.

There were so many lunches and dinners to attend, so many outfits to find, places to visit and people to meet. The year's calendar was overflowing. Best behaviour was essential when mingling and sampling the same favourite canapés as the Duchess of Kent, or waiting to be processed to the top table and seated near to the Princess Royal. Services in St Pauls and many other churches gave opportunities to meet up with friends from other liveries, but being cheeky at Buckingham Palace stays fresh in the memory. Being shown around the Royal Mews brought us to the golden state coach where I asked our guide who was allowed to sit in it. He replied, "Only Royalty," but stepped outside for a breath of air for long enough for me.

A Nature Reserve?

Chris Roome

"There are Humming Bird Hawkmoths and Crested Newts in there," said our new neighbour a few days after we had moved to Staplehurst in 1977. "There" was directly behind both of our gardens - an area consisting of two large ponds, several mature Sycamore and Willow trees, and dense scrub. "There" was in fact the very end of the garden belonging to Vine House, where lived John Silkin MP and his family (LL-SS p206). Our two properties in Jaggard Way in the west, backed on to the mini-wilderness, as did houses at the top of Usborne Close to the north and a bit of Bell Lane to the south. It formed a great backdrop to our garden - a low wooden fence and majestic tall trees and greenery screening us off completely - one of the attractions of the house we had bought as we moved down to Kent from the uplands of Plumstead.

Our neighbour wasn't wrong. There were also Moorhens and Slow-worms, Chiffchaffs and Spotted Flycatchers, Tree Creepers and Great Spotted Woodpeckers, Portuguese Laurel, Butchers' Broom, Primroses and Celandines, beetles and spiders, the occasional fox and the occasional owl. It was a gem and we - freshly down from South London with our very young family - could scarcely believe our luck.

A NATURE RESERVE?

Mr Silkin, a few years later, generously made over the land to Maidstone Borough Council, on condition that it be kept as a Nature Reserve. A committee was formed, work parties organised and the project began to conserve this small wild corner of the village. Bell Lane Nature Reserve became a reality.

Over the next few years, in the 80s, working parties organised by the Bell Lane Reserve Group took place regularly (as they still do). We established what plants were there, noting in particular, Portuguese Laurel - Prunus Lusitanica - a large evergreen shrub with small fragrant white flowers in early summer followed by small dark purple fruits, and Butcher's Broom - Ruscus aculeates - a low evergreen shrub with stiff, spine - tipped leaves. In the past this species was traditionally harvested for its flat and stiff branches to make small brooms that were used for clearing off and cleaning butchering blocks. (Recent research has also established that in addition to this function due to its stiff and spiky leaves, it also exuded previously-unrecognised antibacterial oils which may have contributed to its popularity and common nickname.)

A plethora of tall Sycamores and plenty of Willow around the ponds led to the planting of a Rowan Tree - Sorbus aucuparia - the Mountain Ash, bane of witches and a producer of berries which are good for jam, but better for wild birds - which was why we planted it. This first tree we planted in the reserve is still there and visible from the gate in Bell Lane.

We worked to put up nest boxes, created slender paths and pruned various trees and shrubs to improve habitat and increase the diversity of birds, insects, mammals and plants. Finding a volunteer to tend the bonfire was never a problem in the winter months. We constructed a bird hide between the ponds, but its attraction to teenagers was too tempting for their safety in the dark. I look back with a mix of incredulity at my stupidity and relief at my survival to a memory of standing in wellies in two

feet of water in one of the ponds, using an electric chainsaw on one of the willows, connected to the mains in our house in Jaggard Way, via four plugged-together extension cables! I don't recall goggles, gloves, helmet etc. However, no one commented adversely on the wisdom of this strategy as I cut the big branch and came away unharmed.

During most years the ponds would completely dry out by late summer and be replenished by winter rains. The trees and shrubs and the understory would remain green and fresh however and provide good habitat for wildlife.

Later in the 80s, connections with the school led to teachers taking groups of children to visit the reserve to look hard, to listen hard, to dip the ponds, to collect leaves and creepy crawlies and - above all - to stimulate the children's creative responses to the site through writing and art-making back in school, *"Let Nature be your Teacher – One impulse from a vernal wood – May teach you more of man – of moral evil and of good – than all the sages can."* (William Wordsworth knew what he was writing about.)

A NATURE RESERVE?

As Bell Lane used to house the village blacksmiths' forge and workshop, I have often wondered if these ponds at the top of the small hill on which the medieval centre of the village stands, were created so that carts and wagons, whilst perhaps waiting for horses to be shod, could rest in the ponds to allow their wooden wheels to swell and re-tighten the joints in the rims and axles. Whatever; the ponds now sit firmly in the small reserve, a fragment of space for nature, gifted by John Silkin's generosity and looked after by a dedicated group of volunteers for the last 40 years. Its presence is a heartening reminder of the power of community and action, a reminder of the long and complex past of this settlement in the Weald, and an ever more important witness to the importance of the natural world as we face together the challenges arising from climate change and increased demands for land and homes. Thanks go to the present committee who keep Bell Lane Nature Reserve going. Long may it continue!

Marden Road

Malcolm Buller

In the 1880s, two blocks of three houses were built beside the quiet lane to Marden by the Beechings who ran the Bell Inn. Mr Shoebridge was one of the workmen and he moved in to number 11 where his daughter still lived when we moved in next door on March 31st 1978. We'd bought for nearly £16,000 from Dave O'Brien who needed the money to finish his house in Eire. Later we found out that it had been on the market for two years. Evidence of their animals was everywhere, but the chicken manure in the garden grew fantastic peas and runner beans. At number 15 was a real gentleman, Gus Penfold, who eventually plucked up courage to tell us that we had a shared water supply and when we used the washing machine or hose pipe, he had none. With a large lounge/diner, bathroom and kitchen only on the ground floor, with four bedrooms on the two floors above, we decided that we would make the best we could of things and find somewhere better soon.

Although Marden Road was still a fairly quiet lane, I put up gates just to ensure the boys stopped before they went into the road to fetch a ball. On a couple of occasions, I was called out to render first-aid as cars hit a cyclist and motor-cyclist at the junction with Thatcher Road. Road works there proved entertaining as a water main shower surprised motorists with their windows down, but gave pleasure to the boys on bikes. We wondered how far the workman got blown out of his boots.

MARDEN ROAD

The gasworks had come to the Marden Road in the nineteenth century and were added to in the next. A pair of cottages housed the workers and in 1939 a brick air-raid shelter was built close to the western boundary. It was 2.25 metres long, 2.10m wide with 1.65m vertical walls with an arched roof above. The walls were 35cm thick with a blast wall built to protect the entrance. In 2006, Rowan New Homes asked Victor Smith to write a report on this shelter before they could build the dwellings now known as Maxted Close. He recommended it be retained as it was of unusual design, of historic interest and would make a good garden shed. The round gas holder had already been dismantled in July 1979.

MARDEN ROAD

After a long fight for permission, we engaged Peter Worsley and his brother-in-law, Richard Watts, to build an extension on top of the carport to give us a bathroom and third bedroom on the middle floor with a walk-in attic above. We block-paved the drive, only for the gas company to inform us a few days later that they were going to dig it up to fit in a new main and meter box on the outside. I told them they could not and suggested where they could put it, which they did.

Having become firmly embedded in village life (LL-SS p235) and with both sons through university and married, we decided to move from the now busy Marden Road. It was a long trek to Silverwood beside the even busier Station Road, where in the 70s, with its large garden next to an orchard, Joan had been invited by Gus's friend, Victoria Lockwood, to bring the boys to play, and who had supplied us with a holly tree to plant in front of our house.

MARDEN ROAD

We moved out of The Hollies on December 10th 2010 when our short-term solution of over 31 years came to an end.

My Personal Journey

Reverend Silke Tetzlaff
Rector of All Saints Church in Staplehurst

I would like to take you on a journey. Let me share some events and experiences that have shaped my life and influenced my search for meaning. These moments have guided and impacted on me.

To start, let me tell you about my upbringing in the German Democratic Republic. I was born in Rostock in 1967, six years after the construction of the Berlin Wall. Rostock, a bustling port city on the Baltic Sea, was where I spent my childhood. Watching ferries sail to Denmark from the beach with friends was a common pastime. We often speculated about their destinations, dreaming of boarding one ourselves. However, the reality of the divided world we lived in made such journeys impossible. The presence of soldiers and the risk of crossing the sea made it clear that the dream of exploring the rest of the world was distant. Early on, I grappled with the notion of living in a divided world. Conversations with my family, especially my parents, helped shape my understanding of humanity beyond borders. Despite the restrictions on freely expressing religious beliefs, my parents exemplified love and compassion through their actions, instilling in me the values of love your neighbour as yourself.

MY PERSONAL JOURNEY

Growing up, free creative expression was not encouraged. A memory from an art class stands out, where my unconventional depiction of a road led to an unexpected lesson on realism and creativity. This experience, and others like it, highlighted the challenges of expressing oneself in a constrained environment. As I navigated the complexities of faith and personal beliefs, I found solace in the Lutheran community and committed myself to a life guided by God. Baptism and confirmation marked a significant turning point, reinforcing my faith and conviction in unseen truths.

The fall of the Berlin Wall in 1989 held profound significance for me. It symbolized a moment of unity and hope, a glimpse of a world unburdened by divisions. The collective prayers, protests, and acts of courage leading up to this historic event showcased the power of solidarity and faith in effecting change. As we reflect on the past and look towards a future of unity, may we continue to dismantle walls that divide us, brick by brick, in pursuit of a shared vision of peace, unity and one world.

Always Changing

Malcolm Buller

The connections between the past and present have become very apparent to me over the researching, writing, compilation and editing of residents' tales for these two volumes of 'Staplehurst Stories' during the last eighteen months. The place has influenced the people who in turn have influenced the place.

ALWAYS CHANGING

ALWAYS CHANGING

ALWAYS CHANGING

Often accused of just being a commuter village, residents have demonstrated that those who embrace what is on offer within the community, share their expertise and show they care, all benefit throughout their life here. From the Slaughterhouse Fields, where residents hand-picked peas, grew the Offens Drive link through the Parade of shops to the Tickner and Emerton estate of the 1960s. When we came in 1978 we joined in; took advantage of what was on offer; met interesting people; made friendships that would aid us when in trouble; learnt what made this village special. That involvement led us to join committees, the Parish Council's many strands of work and, where we saw needs, set up new groups with other like-minded folk. We can only hope that those here now and come in the future will make the time and effort to be fully-involved residents. Buildings may stand for centuries, but we all have to pass on the mantle one day.

ALWAYS CHANGING

Iden Manor, Staplehurst.

From The Garden

Malcolm Buller

They called it the Garden of England,
    this county we love and call Kent.
It used to be covered in orchards,
    but no one knows where they all went.
To provide ale for the pubs
    there were gardens of hops
and acres and acres of fields
    for fresh veg for the shops.
Then up there in Whitehall (the land of the toffs)
    some geezer developed a master plan.
He thought that we needed millions of houses.
    "Here! Here!" politicians said to the man.
"Where's closest to Europe?" one asked,
    "Cos Europe's the best place to be.
We need lots of land for our roads and
    'twould be grand if they led to the sea!"
"Now hang on, let's listen to Boris
    and hear what he might have to say.
I think that he thinks that's a bad 'un.
    We should tell 'em all – go away!"

FROM THE GARDEN

They dillied and dallied and dithered
    (as often's the case in the city)
but developers' eyes (not a surprise)
    saw loopholes without any pity.
The Councillors hadn't the courage
    to defend or protect all their lands.
They hadn't a false leg to stand on
    so they swore and sat back on their hands.
The locals could see what was coming;
    the writing was clear on the wall.
'Goodbye to the Garden of England.'
    "Can we move?" "Not a chance - none at all."
The orchards were ripped out for houses
    with tarmac between left and right.
The neighbours were so close together,
    next-door could turn off your light.
Each house had just 1.4 spaces
    to fit in each family's cars.
To escape from the noise and the traffic
    – do a crime. There's more room behind bars!

Written in 2020, this poem was published in the Kent Messenger and Staplehurst Parish Magazine. It resonated with many people.

Staplehurst School

Year 6 Pupils

I visited Staplehurst Primary School to speak to the Year Six pupils and invite them to contribute to this volume of stories. I showed them a copy of 'Listening Lines – Staplehurst Stories' and mentioned the names of some of the previous year's pupils whose work had been included. I asked which hobbies were important to them and they suggested a great variety. We discovered that a hobby could also be a bird or joined with a horse. Finally, writing was mentioned and I was able to show them the published novels and poetry books that I had produced. I stressed how using simple words could be very powerful and funny. I asked how to spell 'I' and said that I spelt it 'eye' and 'see' could be that wet and wavy water. I read them my poem 'Eyesore' which begins, "I saw a saw soar high into the sky with my sore eye and wondered why." which they enjoyed.

The following stories and poems have reached me just in time for them to be included. These are the pupils whose education was severely disrupted by the Covid pandemic and I am grateful for the staff's cooperation in facilitating this.

Playing Cricket - Jake

I can remember the first time I picked up a cricket ball. Ever since then, cricket has been one of my favourite sports. I play for my local club too. It started then. I went to training and it was awesome. My first bowl was alright, but I can do much better now that I've taken this as one of my hobbies. I can also remember my first match, with the bat and the ball. I've taken lots of my time playing for fun. I play matches most weeks and have training every week.

As I bowled for the first time, the moment the ball left my hand I knew it felt great. The ball flew across the rectangle and bounced right where I wanted it. Bouncing up, it almost hit the wickets - the batter didn't get near it. My first wicket was better; it bounced up and hit the top of the stumps. The batter had tried to hit it up, but they missed it. Now I play most days in my garden.

My Life With Horses - Annalise

When I was little, I got attached to horses and as I got older, I got on a huge horse. My heart was beating against my chest; scared in case I fell off and wondering what will happen. When I was young, I watched my older cousin riding a horse and wanted to too. It was so much fun, I loved it so much. I had a horse, a little Shetland called Polly Legs; she was so nice. Now I am really good at horse riding. I drive horses in carts and go travelling a lot on wagons and on horses. I have been travelling ever since I was a child. My first time in a wagon was when I was a baby. I go travelling in trailers all the time. We go every year. This year I went to Appleby's horse fair. It was my first time and I loved it!

My Hobbies - Oliver

Something to do?
Makes you happy?
Why don't you find
Yourself a hobby?
      Outside, the crows are cawing,
      This one isn't the worst,
      I like drawing
      It's my very first.
Head it, flick it, score a goal,
Hurry up, you're being beckoned,
I enjoy playing football,
This sport is my second.
      Come on, smash the wicket!
      This is not absurd,
      I play cricket,
      And it's my third.
Want to collect something real?
That glides back and forth,
I love Hot Wheels,
And they're my fourth.
      Been a long day at school?
      It isn't a myth,
      Gaming is very cool,
      And is also my fifth.
Sport, sci-fi or spooks,
My final hobby, and my sixth,
I like books,
Which are my sixth.
      Relaxing or energetic?
      My poem has come to an end,
      They are all epic,
      They are my hobbies, my friend.

First Swimming Lesson - Jayden

Today I am going swimming in Cranbrook, instead of working after lunch like everyone else in the school is going to do. This is my first lesson; I am excited but pretty nervous. The coach is coming in five minutes. It hopefully will be very large, but I doubt it will be a double-decker. I have brought my swimming bag with everything I need: my shorts, my towel and my swimming goggles, that should be enough. The coach has arrived and it is massive! There are lots of seats at the back, there are five in a row. As I get onto the coach, I fill in from the front and the view is amazing; I haven't been on a coach in years! On my way there, I was chatting for ages and when we arrived, I was stunned. The pool is gigantic. There were three groups, shallow end, deeper end and deepest end. To get sorted into our groups we had to swim a length of the pool doing front crawl and backstroke. I tried but I couldn't do it, so I was put in the shallow end group. Even though I was in this group, it was still loads of fun! We were using floats, going underwater, everything! At the end we were able to play with beach balls and I was playing catch and piggie in the middle with my friends. It was such a great experience.

Journalling - Samah

After a long hard day,
I do journalling every day.
    My mind is overflowing,
    My ideas are ongoing.
My drawings are bad,
It doesn't make me sad.
    I have all the freedom,
    And all the wisdom.
The pages are colourful,
My thoughts are wonderful!

Football - Lewis

Football is my all-time favourite sport. I love playing with my friends because when we play together as a team, we are unstoppable. My dream is to play in the premier league and especially play for my favourite club, Crystal Palace. Crystal Palace is the team that I have supported throughout my entire life, and they are an amazing club with fantastic players. I'm very lucky because I've got the players' autographs and I have pictures with them. I don't just support a club, I play for one. My home club is the Staplehurst Monarchs. I play for the under 11s with my team full of great players, half of them being my friends from school. My team is very good and we have won 2 trophies. 1 of them was for winning the league and the other one was for winning a tournament. I play back and I am good in the position. One time the player had the ball and he was just standing there. No one was tackling him, so I rushed at him and took the ball off of him, nutmegged him and ran with the ball towards the goal, only having to take on the keeper. I ran at the goal with speed, flicked the ball over the keeper and the ball was heading straight for the net, but it hit the crossbar, so I headed it in.

Singing - Abiel

Abiel had always loved singing. She sang everywhere, at every place, all day, every day. When a bad day would come, she would quietly hum to herself, turning into a song of her own. She had been singing in front of many people many times… until she stopped. She stopped singing in front of the crowds. She felt sad as she had become too shy. She was never shy. Until … she plucked up the courage to SING!

When the day came, she felt a little tingly. Stage fright was taking over her. If she didn't control it soon then everything would be over. She stared at the wall and sang like no one was watching. When she finished, a smile (which was impossible to wipe off) crept across her face. She exited the stage, feeling immensely proud.

My hobby Is Singing - Abiel

My hobby is singing,
Winging on the wing,
On an eagle that flies high,
Higher than the sky.
 My hobby is singing,
 While peering out of the window,
 And hearing the wind blow,
 While looking at the snow.
My hobby is singing,
And going out,
I sing whatever circumstance,
Even in a drought!
 My hobby is singing,
 On good days and bad,
 Singing is my lifetime hobby,
 Now, what's yours?

Where Are They? - Answers

Malcolm Buller

1 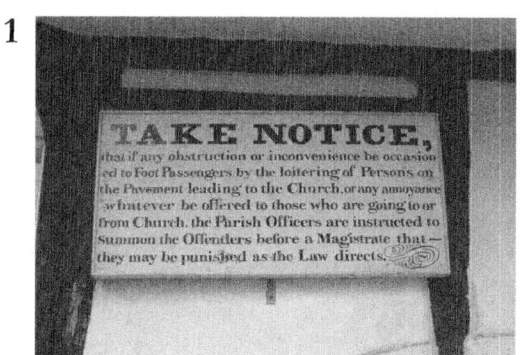 The entrance to All Saints Church used to be narrow as there were matching cottages on both sides. It was not a seemly place for rowdy behaviour as the Notice warns any miscreants.

2  Thousands have passed by this message every day. It is carved into the Memorial to the Marian Martyrs at Cuckolds Corner (LL-SS p90). Unveiled in 1905 and despite collisions, it has survived on this corner of the Marden and Station Roads.

WHERE ARE THEY? - ANSWERS

3 The pair of gates in the High Street have a cobbled footing leading to the drive up to Loddenden Manor. The Usborne family had owned land here since 1473 and inhabited the house from 1534 until 1903.

4 The Ordnance Survey benchmark is the reference point from which maps can be accurately drawn. The limestone surrounding it suggests permanence which is what the old school was from 1873 and the Community Centre probably is for many years to come.

5 The owner of Little Loddenden had paid his fire insurance in 1637 so if a conflagration occurred, his brigade would put it out, but other brigades wouldn't.

WHERE ARE THEY? - ANSWERS

6  This entrance into the 15th century Kings Head was bricked up in 1671 by George and Ann Brown. In 2024 this is the only surviving public house in the parish which used to boast five inns within two hundred yards; 'The LAMB tolled the BELL, knocked the CROWN off the KING'S HEAD which rolled down the hill into the OAK'.

7  The Crown Inn's stabling was accessed along the track which also led to the windmill (LL-SS p170). When the doodlebug struck in 1944, severe damage was caused. This door, with its modern Yale lock, retains a simple bell-pull system and a 'Judas Hole' to see who is outside.

8  When the alleyway to the south of Hill House was incorporated into the building, the window frame had a letterbox built into it. When it was a school this meant the Headmaster had post delivered to his desk

WHERE ARE THEY? - ANSWERS

9

The gasworks holder and cottages were beside the Marden Road where Maxted Close has been built. This iron pipe near Thatcher Road, filled with concrete, could have been a vent from the gas main or the remnant of a gas lamp from the days before electricity.

10

This impressive finial sits above the Market Stores, a traditional corner shop which, in 1846, as well as serving nearby residents, catered for those coming to market or the newly opened railway station. In 2024 it sells kebabs.

Acknowledgements

Thank you to:

- All of the supportive story-tellers who have contributed
- The suppliers of photographs to enhance their stories
- All who have suggested stories and other people to contact
- People who have given permission for their tales to be told
- The Staplehurst Society archivists who have helped find documents and photographs to aid research and for inclusion
- Publications and articles from a variety of sources
- Joan for her patience as I typed for hours on end
- Andrew for his expertise in design and publishing

Thank you to the suppliers of images for front and back covers:

Victoria Works, Chapel Lane - Staplehurst Archives
Bus HKE867 - Robin Oakley
Church and Church Cottages - Frank Page
Iden Manor - Malcolm Buller
Bly Court - Malcolm Buller
Mayor of Maidstone - Eric Hotson
View South from Church Tower - Frank Page
The Lamb Cottages - Frank Page

Useful Contacts

For your publishing needs – andrewbuller.co.uk

To add to or enquire of the Staplehurst Archives – staplehurstsociety.org

To contact the author – mpbuller1@btinternet.com

Printed in Great Britain
by Amazon